Master, Mentor, Master

THOMAS COLE & FREDERIC CHURCH

BY JOHN WILMERDING

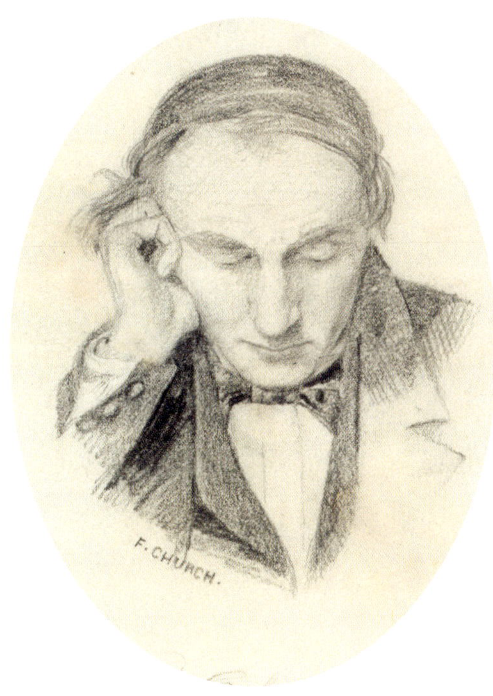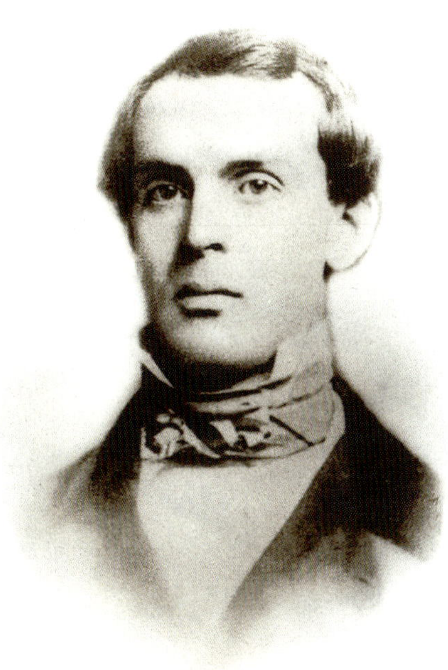

April 30–November 2, 2014

THOMAS COLE NATIONAL HISTORIC SITE
CATSKILL, NEW YORK

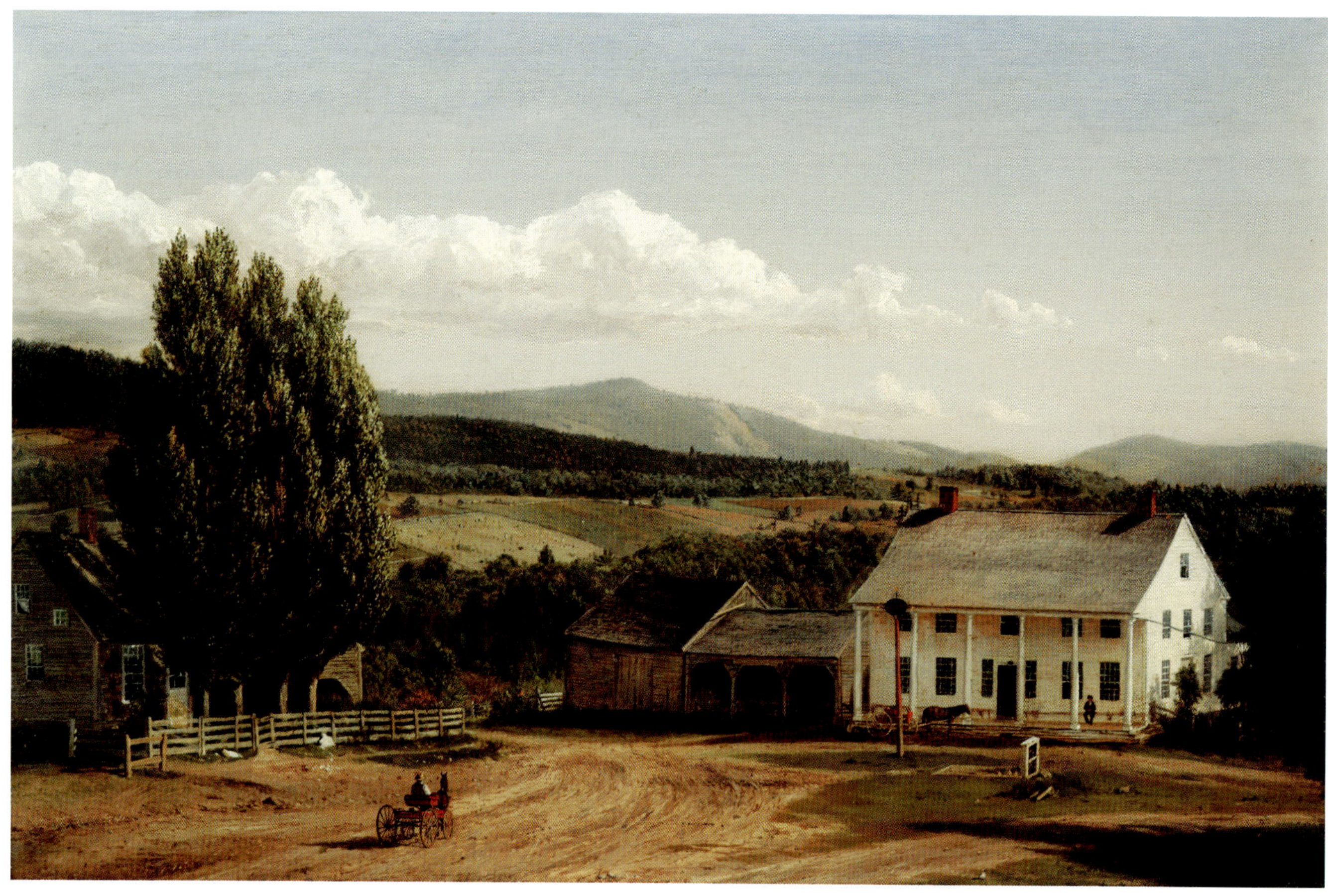

FIG. 1. FREDERIC E. CHURCH, *View in Pittsford, Vermont*, 1848. Oil on academy board, 11 x 16¼ inches. Collection Richard Sharp.

Director's Foreword

OF ALL THE MOMENTOUS EVENTS that have occurred in this 199-year-old house, maybe none had a bigger impact on the history of American art than the 1844 arrival of eighteen-year-old Frederic Church from Hartford. For the next two years, the young artist whom Cole described as having "the finest eye for drawing in the world" grew under Cole's watchful eye. It is interesting to think about what kind of teacher Cole was at that time, with his reputation and career already well-established and, at age forty-three, twenty-five years older than Church. He certainly had been successful in showing his friend Asher B. Durand the ins-and-outs of landscape painting on their 1837 Schroon Lake trip, and his mentoring style with young Church may not have been much different. "I have always treated my students as friends as well as pupils," Cole wrote, and it is clear the feelings fostered by his friendship with Church, who was only twenty-one when Cole died, were deep and long-lasting, even if Cole's life would not be.

That friendship was evident in many ways after Cole's death. Church's painting *To the Memory of Cole* (1848) was the first painted memorial to Cole, even if it did not end up the most famous (see Durand's 1849 painting *Kindred Spirits*). Certainly the bond can be seen in the way Church kept in touch with Cole's widow and family—even employing Cole's son Theddy as the manager of his farm—and advising the family on both the sale and reacquisition of Cole's paintings. But perhaps the greatest and most obvious testament to their friendship is the fact that in 1860, flush with the success of his masterpiece *The Heart of the Andes* and about to be married, Church—who could have chosen to live anywhere in the world—bought Wynson Breezy farm in Hudson, New York, a property just across the river and only two miles from Cole's house. During the 1830s and 1840s, Cole had sketched the breathtaking views from this property, then known as Red Hill, and in May 1845 he introduced Church to the site. Although it is unclear whether Cole accompanied Church on this trip, the fact that the specific view Church sketched is virtually identical to the view Cole always sketched from that site—despite the panoramic expanse the site affords—makes it tempting to imagine the two great artists, student and teacher, friends, sitting side by side as they worked. Construction of Church's elaborate home began in 1870, and over the next several decades he would develop this magnificent property into present-day Olana, calling it "the center of the world."

This year marks the 170th anniversary of Frederic Church's arrival at the Cole House, and today, the relationship between the Persian-style castle on the east side of the Hudson River and the Federal home on the west side is as strong as ever, as manifested in our eleventh annual exhibition. *Master, Mentor, Master: Thomas Cole & Frederic Church* is the first exhibition to explore this crucial moment in American art history. It brings together pivotal early works of Church, as well as key examples by Cole from the same time period, allowing us to see firsthand the sketched and painted evidence of this highly successful artistic tutelage. If Church found the perfect teacher, Cole found the perfect student. It should come as no surprise that the combination of Church's exquisite and unmatched technical expertise with Cole's "higher style" of landscape painting—his insistence on imbuing a scene with the spiritual—would produce the greatest artist of the second half of the nineteenth century.

ELIZABETH B. JACKS, *Director*
Thomas Cole National Historic Site

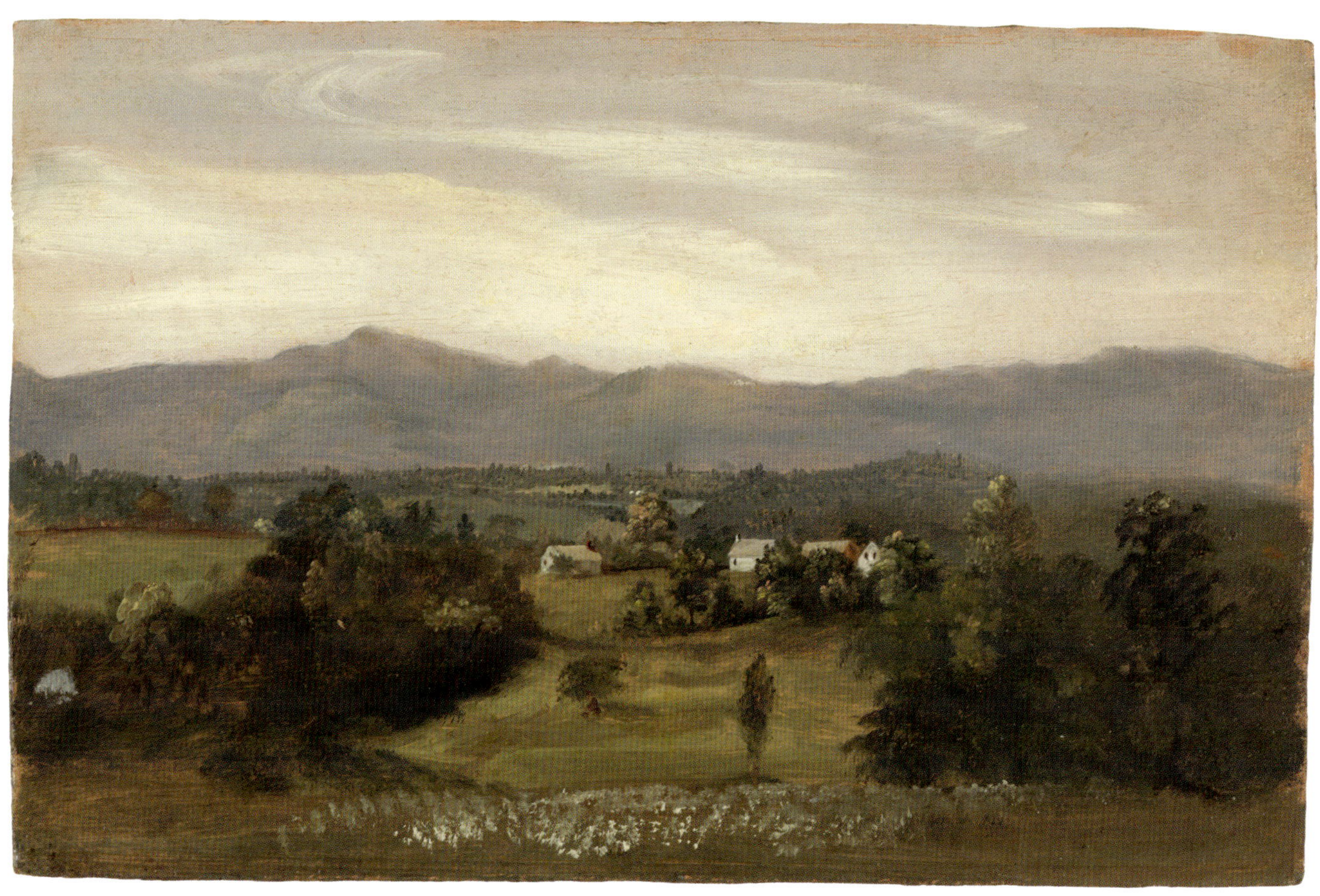

FIG. 2. FREDERIC E. CHURCH, *View of the Catskills from the Hudson River Valley*, c. 1844. Brush and oil paint, graphite on heavy paperboard, 7¹⁵/₁₆ x 11⁷/₈ inches. Cooper-Hewitt, National Design Museum, Smithsonian Institution, New York, NY, Gift of Louis P. Church, 1917-4-333. Photo: Matt Flynn © Smithsonian Institution.

Acknowledgments

WE WOULD LIKE TO EXPRESS our profound appreciation to John Wilmerding for bringing this remarkable exhibition to life. We are grateful to the lenders of the artworks in the exhibition: Albany Institute of History and Art; Michael Altman; Colorado Springs Fine Art Center; Cooper-Hewitt, National Design Museum, Smithsonian Institution; Florence Griswold Museum; National Gallery of Art; The Olana Partnership and Olana State Historic Site, New York State Office of Parks, Recreation and Historic Preservation; Richard Sharp; Washington County Museum of Fine Arts; and anonymous private collectors.

Any significant exploration of the relationship between Thomas Cole and Frederic Church, and this unique moment in art history, is indebted to the prior writing and research of many esteemed scholars, especially Franklin Kelly and Gerald L. Carr. In addition we would like to thank the people and organizations that have assisted with this project: Lisa Hankin, Adelson Gallery; Tammis K. Groft, W. Douglas McCombs, and Tom Nelson, Albany Institute of History and Art; Jon Erickson, Michael Altman Fine Art & Advisory Services; Kevin Avery; Berry-Hill Galleries; Blake Milteer and Michael Howell, Colorado Springs Fine Art Center; Gail S. Davidson, Cooper-Hewitt, National Design Museum, Smithsonian Institution; Jeff Anderson, Amy Kurtz Lansing, and Nicole Wholean, Florence Griswold Museum; Ronna Dixson and Mark Peckham, New York State Office of Parks, Recreation and Historic Preservation; Valerie Balint and Evelyn Trebilcock, The Olana Partnership; Angela Scerbo, Questroyal Fine Art; Patti Junker, Seattle Art Museum; Rebecca Massie Lane, Washington County Museum of Fine Arts; and Sean Morello, Eli Wilner & Co. Additional thanks to Amon Carter Museum of American Art, Brooklyn Museum, Cincinnati Art Museum, The Cleveland Museum of Art, Harvard Art Museums/Fogg Museum, Munson-Williams-Proctor Arts Institute, The Nelson-Atkins Museum of Art, Reynolda House Museum of American Art, Seattle Art Museum, Smithsonian American Art Museum, and Wadsworth Atheneum Museum of Art.

John Wilmerding joins us in thanking the many people above who have made this exhibition and catalogue possible and extends special thanks to Kate Menconeri, assistant curator, for her significant contributions to the research, writing, and selections for this project; Kelsey Hoffman, 2013 Cole fellow, for conducting important early research; and David Barnes, Thomas Cole trustee, for being the spark that began this project. Sincere thanks to Kathleen Luhrs and Rita Lascaro for their impeccable work on the catalogue; Patrick Terenchin for helping to create a beautiful gallery installation; and to our visitors, volunteers, and staff Sheri Dejan, Melissa Gavilanes, Marie Spano, Samantha Singleton, and Alice Tunison for making our events and season such a success.

This exhibition and catalogue are organized by the Thomas Cole National Historic Site with guest curator, John Wilmerding, and assistant curator, Kate Menconeri. The exhibition is made possible by the generous support of the Wyeth Foundation for American Art, Eli Wilner & Co., the Bay and Paul Foundations, the Bank of Greene County, the Greene County Legislature through the County Initiative Program administered by the Greene County Council on the Arts; and the Hudson River Valley National Heritage Area.

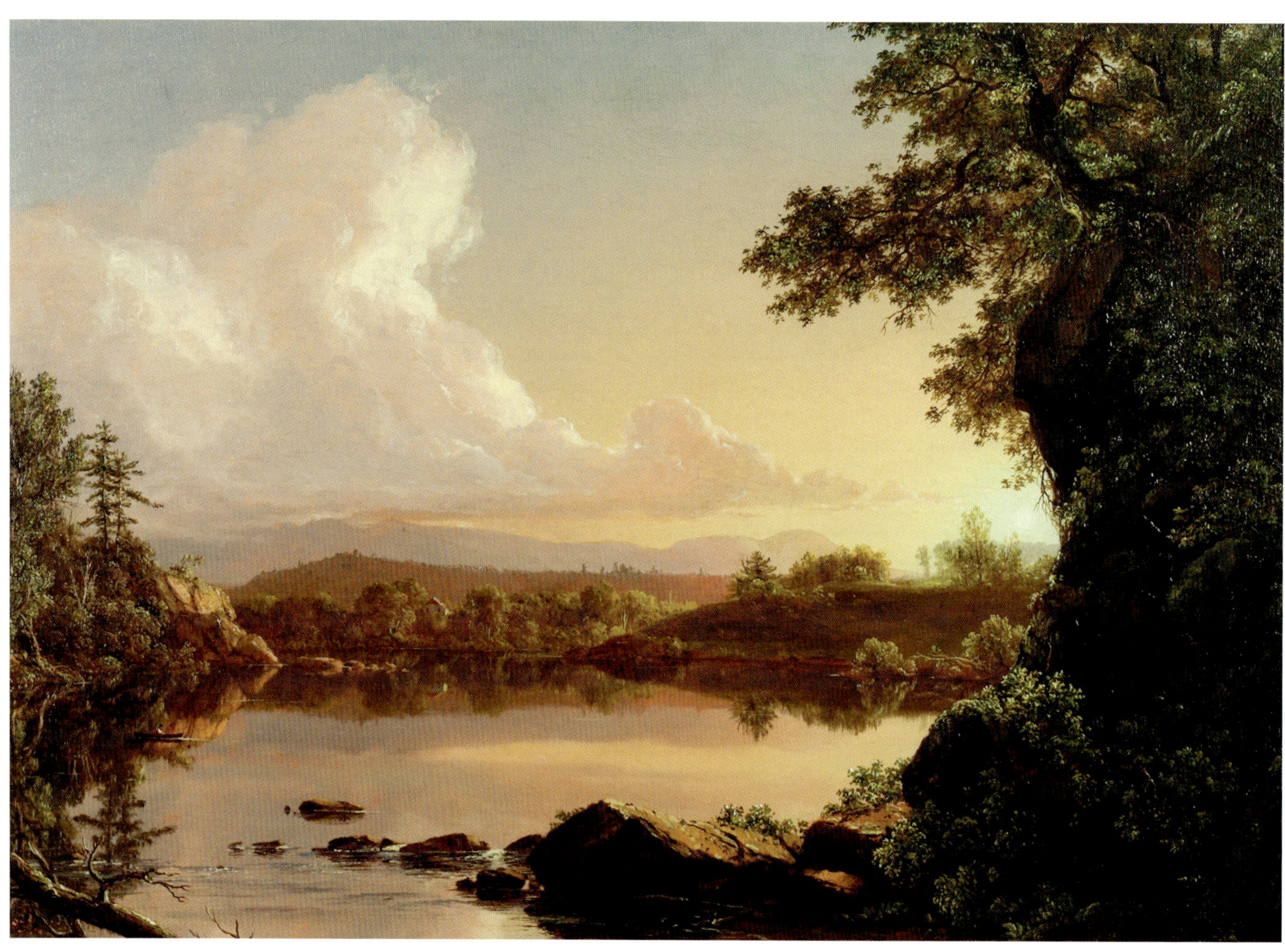

FIG. 3. FREDERIC E. CHURCH, *Scene on Catskill Creek*, 1847. Oil on canvas, 21½ x 29¾ inches. Washington County
Museum of Fine Arts, Hagerstown, MD.

Master, Mentor, Master
THOMAS COLE & FREDERIC CHURCH

BY JOHN WILMERDING

There are a surprising number of major teacher-student relationships in the history of American art. But none was quite as influential and important as that between the founder of the Hudson River School of painters, Thomas Cole (1801–1848), and his student-successor, Frederic Church (1826–1900). One thinks of Benjamin West and Gilbert Stuart in the eighteenth century and of Thomas Hart Benton and Jackson Pollock in the twentieth. Then there are the great family dynasties: Charles Willson Peale with his brother James and son Raphaelle during the early nineteenth century. Dominating much of the twentieth century are the Wyeths, N. C., Andrew, and Jamie. For all of these it is stimulating to speculate the ways in which the student equaled or surpassed the mentor.

The answer is ambivalent with Cole and Church, for both rose to preeminent, though different, roles in American painting. The older artist was one of the earliest to introduce and establish in the young republic the conventions of English landscape painting, and make nature not just a new, but also the dominant, subject for American art through the first half of the nineteenth century. With greater technical abilities and intellectual acuity, the younger man decisively transformed this foundation into a contemporary native vision. Church articulated a pictorial expression of national identity and destiny during the country's great mid-century crisis of the Civil War years and its aftermath. Together, these two artists were the key forces in defining the character and direction of American landscape painting, Cole over the second quarter of the nineteenth century and Church

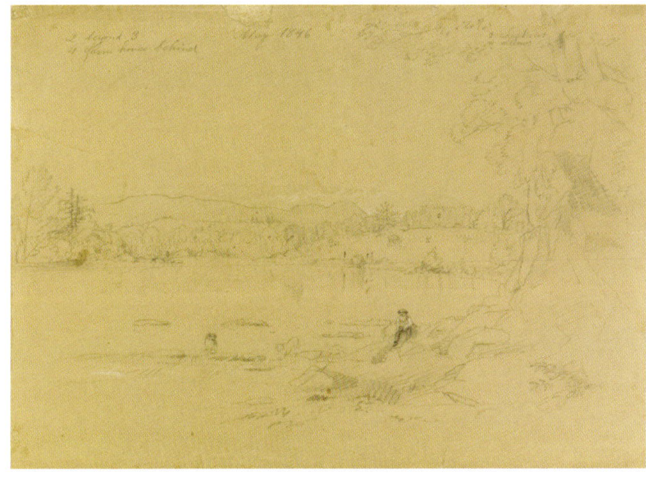

FIG. 4. FREDERIC E. CHURCH, *Catskill Creek*, May 1846. Graphite and chalk on paper, 7 13/16 x 13 5/16 inches. Olana State Historic Site, Hudson, New York State Office of Parks, Recreation and Historic Preservation, OL.1977.293.

over the third quarter. The transition of those ideas crucially began in the two years from 1844 to 1846 when one tutored the other.

Although the lives and works of both figures are generally familiar, some biographical chronology here would be useful as context. Cole was born and grew up in England. As a youth he gained some training in engraving, a practice that would have provided his first introduction to drawing, and he enjoyed walking in the countryside. Like many at this time, his family was soon lured by the prospects of work and making a life in the New World. As a teenager, he moved with his family to Philadelphia in 1818.

Further experience in designing and exposure to portrait painting soon led Cole to contemplate a career as an artist. Settling in New York in 1825 came at a critical time. Not only were there opportunities for sketching in the nearby Hudson Valley, but the opening of the Erie Canal marked the start of unprecedented expansion for trade and immigration to western New York and beyond. Not least, it confirmed the vast new possibilities for painting the American landscape. Three of Cole's paintings were put up for sale in a New York shop window, and were bought by noteworthy contemporaries. Unexpectedly, we could say they represented the past, present, and future. One purchaser was John Trumbull, the great history painter from an earlier generation; the second was William Dunlap, then at work on the first comprehensive history of the artistic practice in the United States, representing the present; and Asher B. Durand (then an engraver), who would outlive Cole by almost four decades and carry the mantle of Hudson River painting (along with Church) through the next generation of landscape artists.

Cole began spending summers in Catskill in the upper Hudson River Valley in 1826, sketching constantly in the surrounding area. Within the next couple of years he established himself as an exemplary interpreter of the American wilderness, creating paintings of recognizable scenes as well as allegorical compositions with lofty historical or religious content. The real and ideal became two parallel tracks in his art, and would become more integrated in the subsequent art of Frederic Church.

By 1829 Cole felt the need to travel, study, and paint abroad. Upon his departure, his friend the nature poet William Cullen Bryant cautioned the artist in a poem not to lose his sensibility for an American idiom, that in being lured to Europe he keep "that wilder image bright." In England he met some of his major contemporaries, including John Constable, Joseph M. W. Turner, and John Martin. All would be influential in Cole's later work. On the Continent, travel around Italy and visits to the great museum collections exposed the young painter to the long traditions of classicism. There the idea came to him for his first great allegorical suite of pictures, *The Course of Empire* (The New-York Historical Society), which he was able to execute on his return to New York,

completing the series in 1836. Their composition owed an obvious debt to Turner and Martin.

But that year was also key in the maturing of his career, for he would paint one of his defining landscape masterpieces, *View from Mount Holyoke, Northampton, Massachusetts, after a Thunderstorm—The Oxbow* (The Metropolitan Museum of Art). This by contrast descended from the plein-air scenes of Constable. Now Cole had set forth archetypal examples of both idealized philosophical paintings along with charged recordings of actual identifiable sites. While his exhibition of *The Course of Empire* received praise, his ambitions for allegorical painting had a mixed reception, so in 1841 he embarked on a return trip to Europe. This resulted in views of Mount Etna from Taormina and the stone ruins stretching across the Roman campagna, meditations on the lost classical past. Church would later redo the Mount Etna composition in his own rendering of the New World volcano Cotopaxi in the northern Andes.

Once back in New York, Cole turned more intensely to religious painting. In 1844 he wrote to the collector Daniel Wadsworth in Hartford, Connecticut, "I have been dwelling on many subjects. . . . They are subjects of a moral and religious nature. . . . Another subject under consideration I would call Life, Death and Immortality— a series of three pictures."[1] Torn between celebrating nature at home and contemplating the fall of past empires, he relied on pictorial precedents from earlier European painting even as he sought to adapt them to a nationalist American sensibility. That dilemma would only be fully resolved in his pupil's hands over the years to come. But now Cole was at the height of his reputation and influence. At this point in what was to be the final phase of his shortened life, he agreed to take on a few apprentices, the most notable by far being Frederic Church.

Let us bring the younger aspiring artist's biography forward to this momentous point of convergence. Church was born in 1826 into an old Hartford family, and was said to have shown a youthful talent for drawing and an inclination for an artistic career. His father approached Daniel Wadsworth, the prominent local collector of works by the Revolutionary history painter John Trumbull and patron of Cole's landscapes. At Wadsworth's request, Cole acceded to accepting the teenager, a full generation

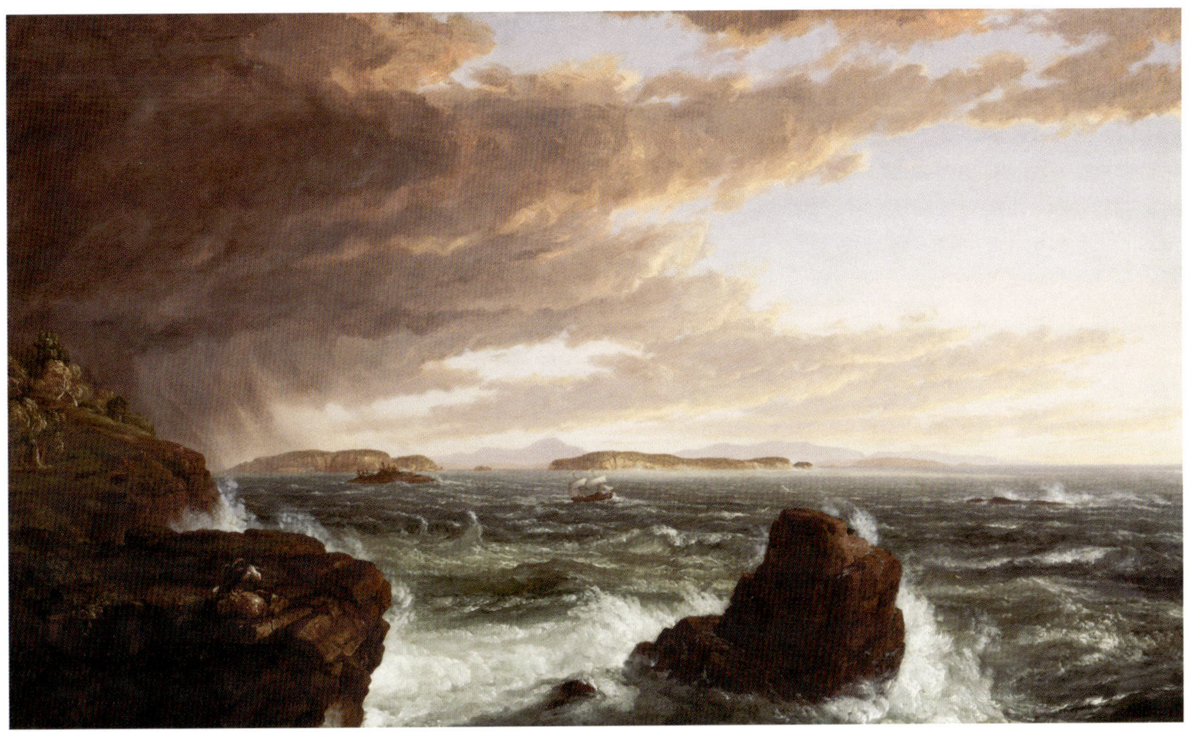

FIG. 5. THOMAS COLE, *View Across Frenchman's Bay from Mt. Desert Island, After a Squall,* 1845.
Oil on canvas, 38⁵/₁₆ x 62⁵/₈ inches. Cincinnati Art Museum, OH, Gift of Alice Scarborough.

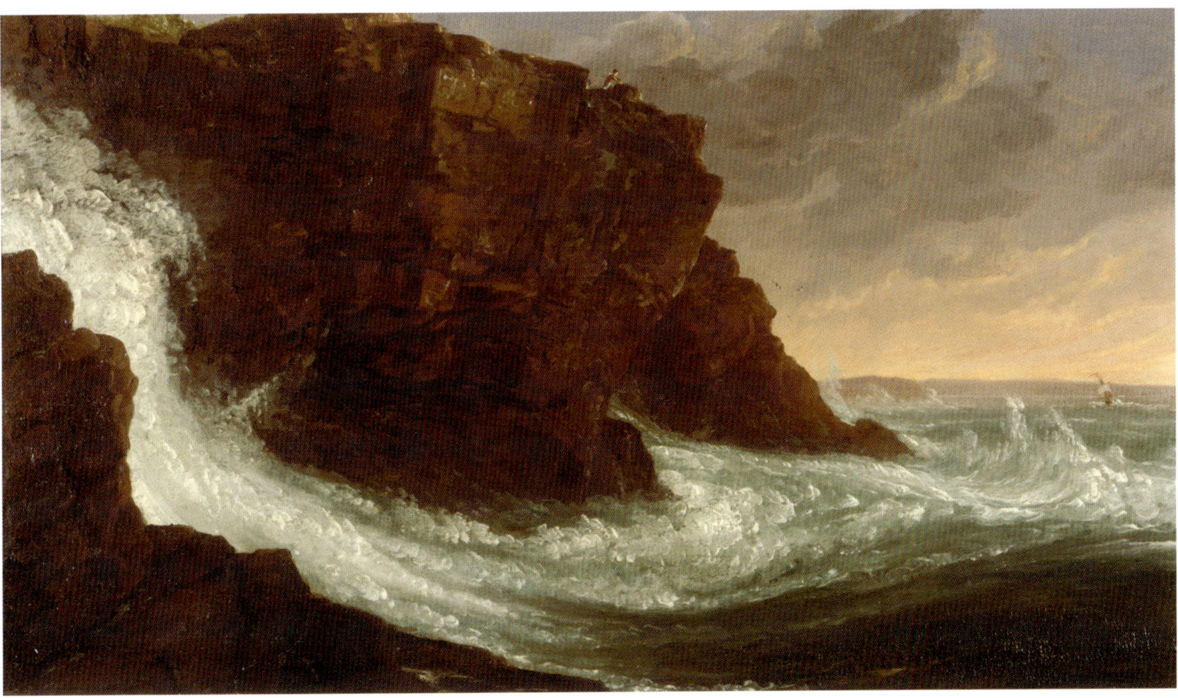

FIG. 6. THOMAS COLE, *Frenchman's Bay, Mount Desert Island, Maine,* 1844. Oil on wood, 14 x 23 inches.
Albany Institute of History and Art, NY.

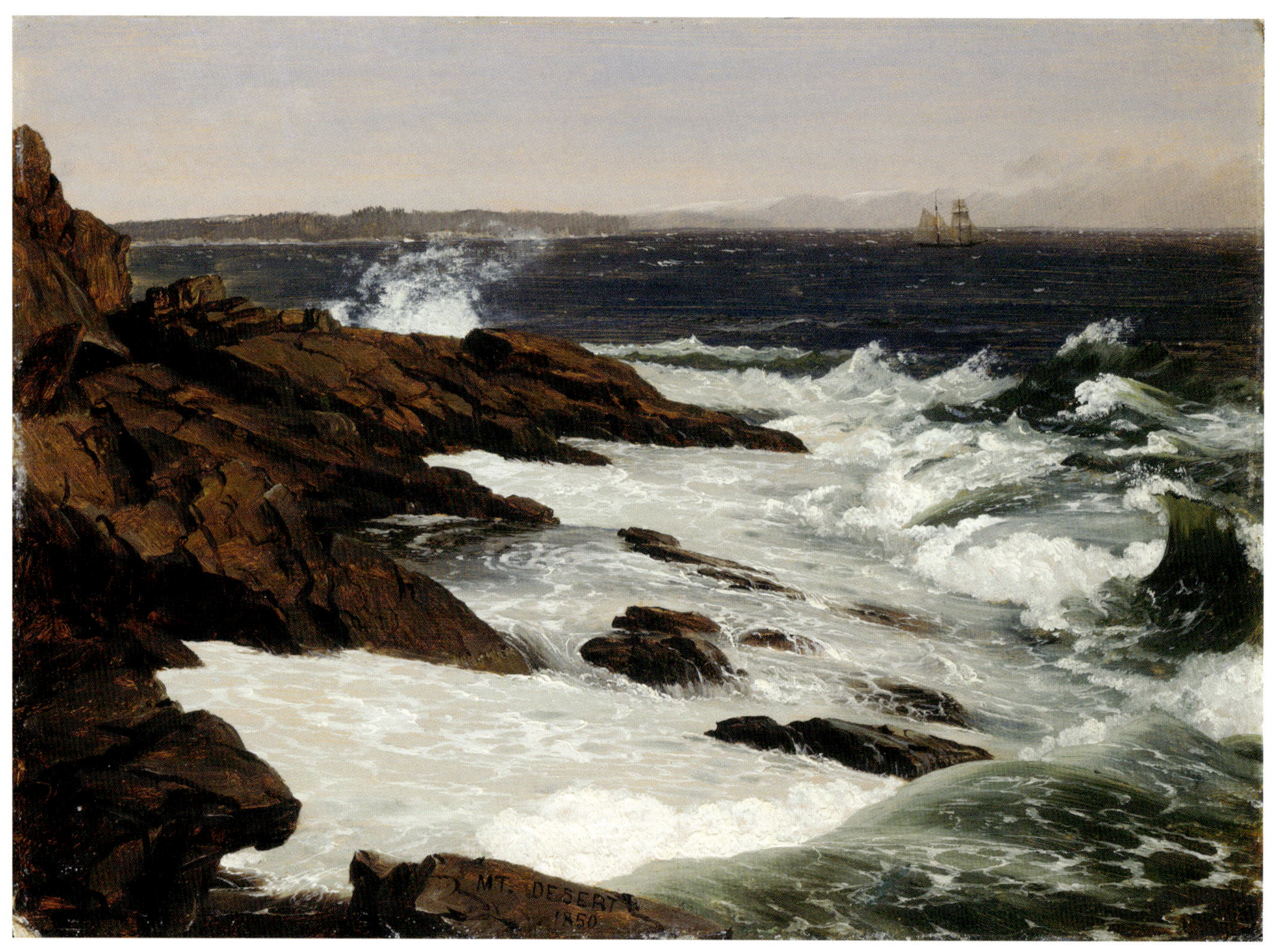

FIG. 7. FREDERIC E. CHURCH, *Fog off Mount Desert*, c. 1850. Oil on academy board, 11½ x 15½ inches. Private collection, promised gift, National Gallery of Art, Washington, DC.

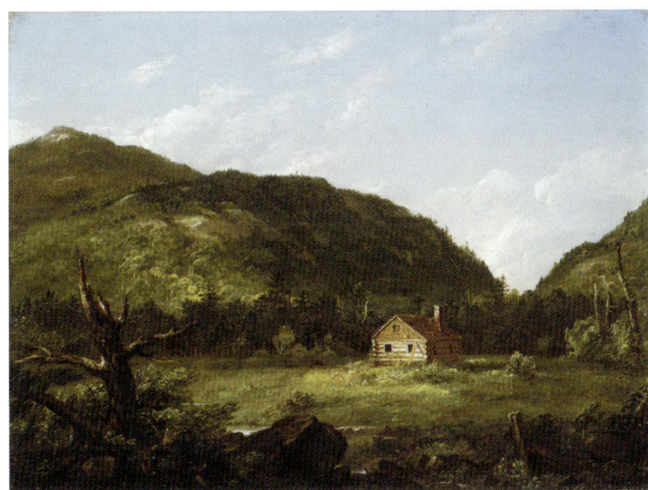

FIG. 8. Thomas Cole, *House, Mount Desert Island, Maine*, 1844–45. Oil on canvas, 18⁹/₁₆ x 24¹/₈ inches. Harvard Art Museums/ Fogg Museum, Cambridge, MA. Transfer from Harvard University, Bequest of Edward Charles Pickering.

younger, as a student. In the older artist's journal is the notation: "Mr. Church came to stay with me on the 4th June 1844. He is to pay me $300 for the year." And below, "Paid his expenses to Hartford–4.25/ Paid for letters–.25" [INSIDE FRONT COVER]. Later that summer in Boston he noted, "I arrived here last evening. I spent a day with Mr. Church at Hartford, very pleasantly."[2]

Before joining Cole, young Church wrote him, "my parents (as well as myself) would prefer that I board with your family."[3] Lodgings, however, were found nearby, though it seems Church also made use of an attic bedroom on the third floor of the Cole house in Catskill. Less than three months after Church's arrival, the older painter set off on a crucial trip to the Maine coast with another painter-friend, Henry Cheever Pratt of Boston. Their route of travel was unusual, overland by buckboard through New Hampshire and central Maine, rather than by vessel along the coast. In his sketchbook, Cole recorded his first views of the hills of Mount Desert Island seen from the north and on August 29 indicated, "We are now at a village in which there is no tavern, in the heart of Mount Desert Island."[4] This was Somesville, one of the oldest settlements on the island, centrally located at the head of a long deep cut of water known as Somes Sound, making possible their excursions to various points inland and to the rugged coastline east and south.

Over the next couple of weeks Cole explored various panoramas. On the rugged eastern shore he recorded, "Sept 3.—The ride here to Lynham's [*sic*] was delightful, affording fine views of Frenchman's Bay on the left, and the lofty peaks of Mount Desert on the right."[5] The Lynam family owned a farm sheltered off a small cove behind Schooner Head, which became in subsequent years a hospitable place for artists to stay and walk the nearby cliffs. One of Cole's most finished drawings in his sketchbook viewed the Porcupine Islands extending off Bar Harbor into Frenchman's Bay.[6] It later resulted in his most ambitious canvas [FIG. 5] depicting Mount Desert scenery.

Although the site is recognizable in the painting, the artist took liberties with the expanse of space he included in the composition. On the left side we are looking north to the islands, while to the right our view is to the southeast and the open ocean. For the sake of dramatic effect Cole has conflated this compass spread into a single scene. In the lower left corner we note an eagle perched on the rocky promontory. This also fused several references together. To be sure, bald eagles were a common site over the island, as they are again today, but were also of artistic interest to Cole's contemporaries. One figures prominently in Charles Willson Peale's late masterpiece, *The Artist in His Museum*, 1823 (Pennsylvania Academy of the Fine Arts), and not long before Cole's visit, the ornithologist painter John James Audubon had passed through the area and recorded the eagle for his great project, *The Birds of America*. In addition, Cole was certainly alluding to the bird as a national symbol, investing his scene with moral purpose and grandeur.

From the trip at least three other oils resulted. One major work completed in the same year as his travels is *Frenchman's Bay, Mount Desert Island, Maine*, 1844 [FIG. 6]. The small lone figure atop the cliff speaks to Cole's sense of the sublime and echoes his letter to his wife, Maria:

> a tremendous overhanging precipice, rising
> from the ocean, with the surf dashing against
> it in a frightful manner. The whole coast along
> here is iron bound—threatening crags, and dark
> caverns in which the sea thunders.[7]

Another was probably the picture Cole's biographer Louis Legrand Noble referred to as "Sea View," painted in 1845. It shows the precipitous rock wall along today's Ocean Drive known as Otter Cliffs. Again Cole arbitrarily made adjustments in its profile to convey the awesome drama of the location. In the painting we observe its silhouette with open water on the right, a view in actuality impossible to obtain. (The reverse is in fact what one can see.) He also tilts the cliff face forward, whereas it is really a vertical drop, and places a small figure at its top, all to augment a sense of sublime power and man dwarfed in this wilderness setting.

More modest in scale, *House, Mount Desert Island, Maine* [FIG. 8], a scene Cole described to Noble: "we came to a romantic place near a mountain gorge, with a house and a piece of meadow."[8] Set within the island's interior is a rustic log cabin framed by the rising hills on either side, an embodiment of domestic settlement within nature's virgin forest. It would prove to be an image that engaged Church intensely in the years ahead.

We can only imagine the excitement and interest the young apprentice must have felt on Cole's return to Catskill, showing the drawings he had made in Maine, and turning them into paintings over the following year. It is no accident that after Cole's death a few years later his former pupil set off to visit Mount Desert, where he made a point of seeking out many of the locales Cole had seen and drawn, such as *Fog off Mount Desert,* 1850 [FIG. 7]. During the two years of Church's tutelage, the older artist introduced him to much of the terrain near Catskill, providing subjects that both of them painted. Cole often ventured out on his own, leaving at home the young man, who served as both informal older brother and babysitter to the Cole children. To his wife on March 3, 1845, Cole wrote, "I forgot to tell the children they must be very good when I am away. I hope Theddy draws, and Mary. Ask Mr. Church if he will not give Theddy a little lesson. Tell Mr. C that I expect to see something quite fine on my return." In addition, Cole also offered technical hints about sketching and painting, but early on realized how fine a draftsman was emerging in his tutee, proclaiming Church "has the finest eye for drawing in the world."[9]

Church's lifelong connection to his mentor, and to Cole's family, is evidenced by his many sketches and letters to them, the latter which continue well into the second half of the century. One of the first landscapes that eighteen-year-old Church made under Cole was probably from a vantage point close to Cole's house. The peaks of the Catskills including High Peak and Round Top, as well as the Catskill Mountain House are clearly identifiable in *View of the Catskills from the Hudson River Valley* [FIG. 2]. His sketch, *Catskill Creek,* May 1846 [FIG. 4], depicts a similar view, and even includes Cole's young son Theddy and his dog Tiger. From this graphite drawing, Church made the finished oil painting *Scene on Catskill Creek,* 1847 [FIG. 3].[10] Cole's influence is evident in the depiction of the pastoral side of nature, but Church's clear and exacting attention to nature's details and precise light sets this work apart from that of his mentor.[11] The same might be suggested of *July Sunset* [FIG. 9], which also pictures Catskill Creek and a boy thought to be Cole's son. The painting is one of two that Church sent for exhibition at the National Academy of Design in the spring of 1847, and a writer at the time compared its composition to Cole's *Schroon Lake,* asserting that the painting was strongly influenced, if not made, by Cole himself.[12]

Another early oil study by Church, *Hudson River with Factory by Moonlight,* 1845 [FIG. 10], pictures a factory Church would have encountered along the river at this time. It is compelling both for its dramatic and almost celestial atmosphere of billowing smoke under a moonlit sky, as well as for its truth. While Cole rarely depicted the industry that was already bustling in the 1840s Hudson River Valley environs, Church painted what he saw, as instructed by his mentor. "Cole told him [Church] to go out and paint what he pleased and how he pleased, but advised him to try simple things and do them as thoroughly and truthfully as possible."[13] There were several foundries listed in Hudson, New York, by 1851, including one owned by the family of fellow painter Sanford Gifford. Olana's curators see this work as a precursor to Church's renderings of erupting volcanoes in South America and the signature atmospheric effects for which he would later become known.[14]

Between 1844 and 1846 Cole painted a number of his best-known works, including *The Cross in the Wilderness* [FIG. 25], *The Mountain Ford, Campagna*

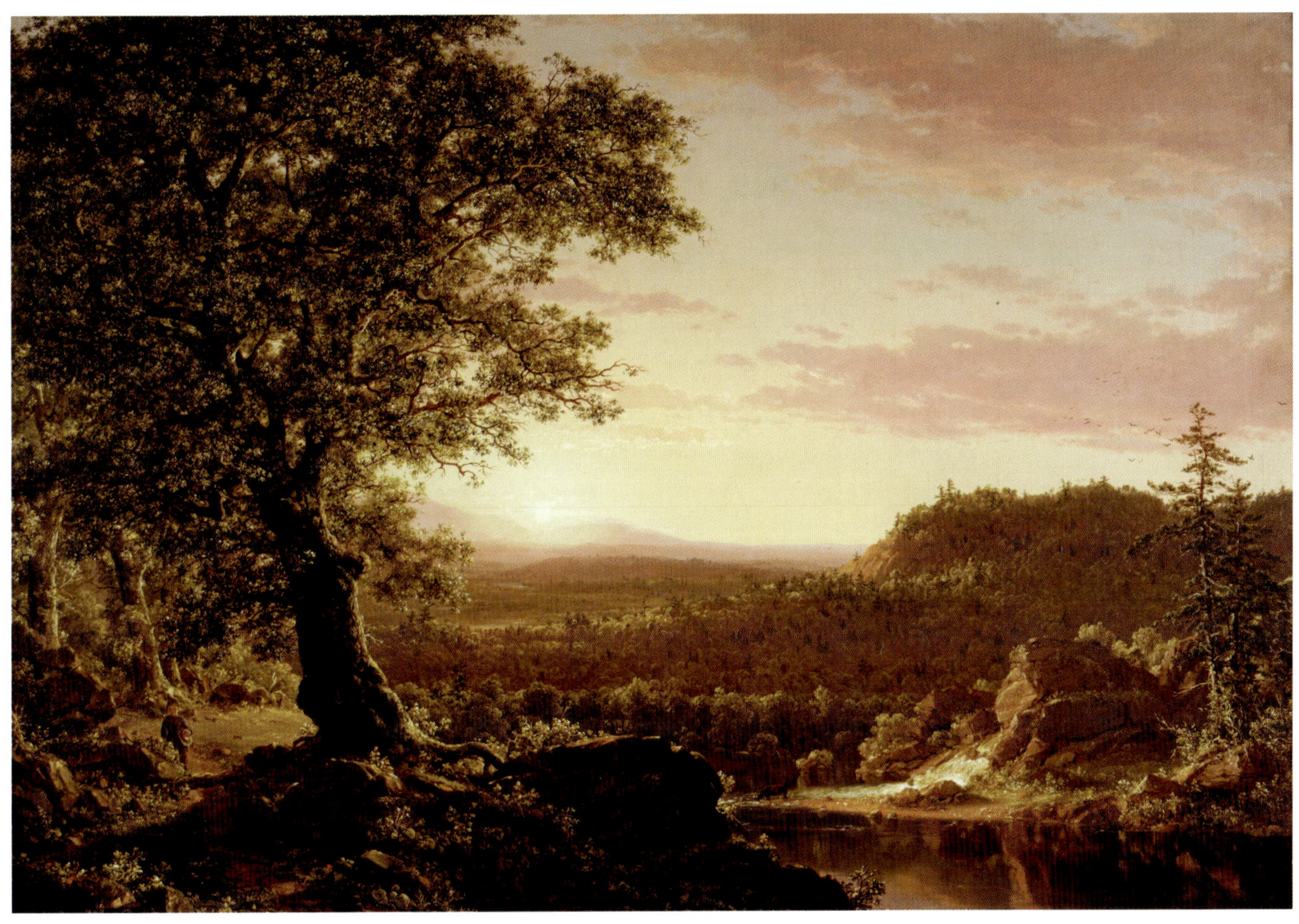

FIG. 9. FREDERIC E. CHURCH, *July Sunset*, 1847. Oil on canvas, 29 x 40½ inches. Private collection.

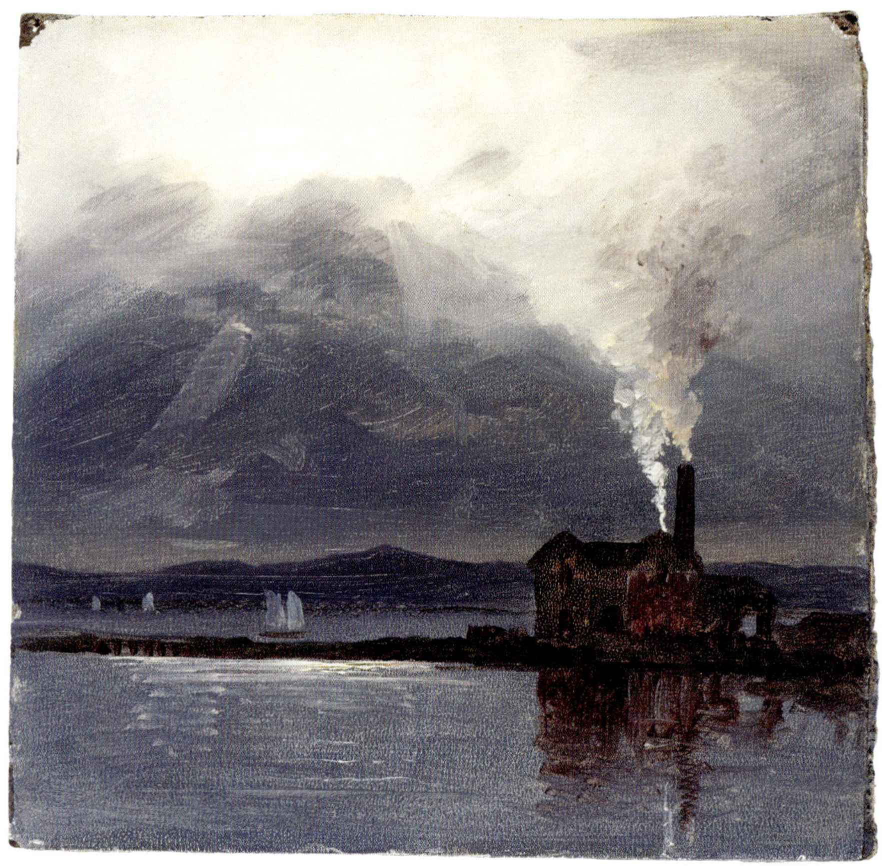

FIG. 10. FREDERIC E. CHURCH, *Hudson River with Factory by Moonlight*, 1844–45. Brush and oil on paperboard, 8 11/16 x 8 15/16 inches. Cooper-Hewitt, National Design Museum, Smithsonian Institution, New York, NY, Gift of Louis P. Church, 1917-4-44. Photo: © Smithsonian Institution.

di Roma, *Catskill Mountain House*, *L'Allegro*, and *Il Penseroso*. As the titles indicate, these were a mix of allegorical pictures, remembered European sites, and freshly observed American views. Near the end of the period Cole produced *The Pic-Nic Party* [FIG. 20], which Noble pronounced "a sylvan scene, all American." [15] It was unusual in its fusion of landscape and genre. This narrative underpinning continued to the end of Church's stay at Catskill with *Home in the Woods* and *The Hunter's Return* [FIGS. 21 AND 18], an important theme of civilization intersecting with wilderness that Church would pursue in the immediate years after leaving Cole.

At this time Cole not only worked on familiar Catskill vistas, but also landscapes suffused in dramatic effects of weather and light, for example, intense summer twilights that had an indelible impact on Church and led to his signature series of increasingly intense sunset canvases during the 1850s. Noble declared one twilight scene on the Catskill River by Cole [FIG. 13] "among his finest landscapes" and poetically described its effect as "the delicate skirt of a brilliant summer afternoon." [16] The vivid skies for which Church would become famous can be traced to early works such as *Sunrise*, 1847 [FIG. 14]. Gerald Carr has related this vibrant sky, most likely a view from the Catskill Mountain House where Cole and Church often journeyed, to *July Sunset*, 1847; *Morning, Looking East over the Hudson Valley from the Catskill Mountains*, 1848 [FIGS. 9 AND 15]; and the artist's later works, including *Twilight (Mount Desert Maine)*. [17]

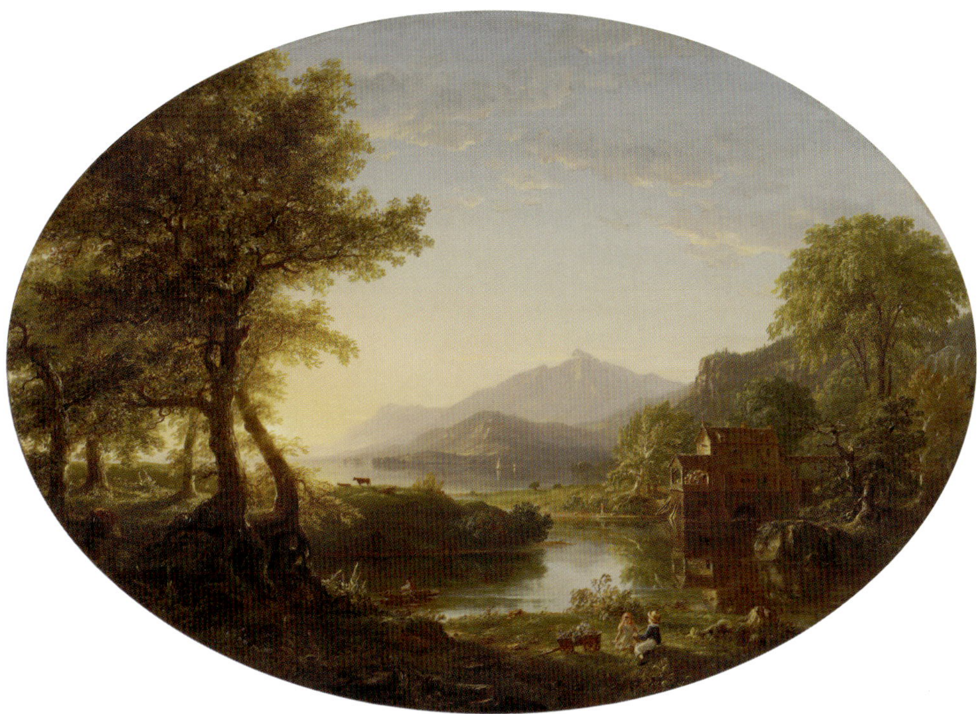

FIG. 11. THOMAS COLE, *The Mill, Sunset*, 1844. Oil on canvas, 26 ⅛ x 36 1/16 inches. The Nelson-Atkins Museum of Art, Kansas City, MO. Photo: Jamison Miller.

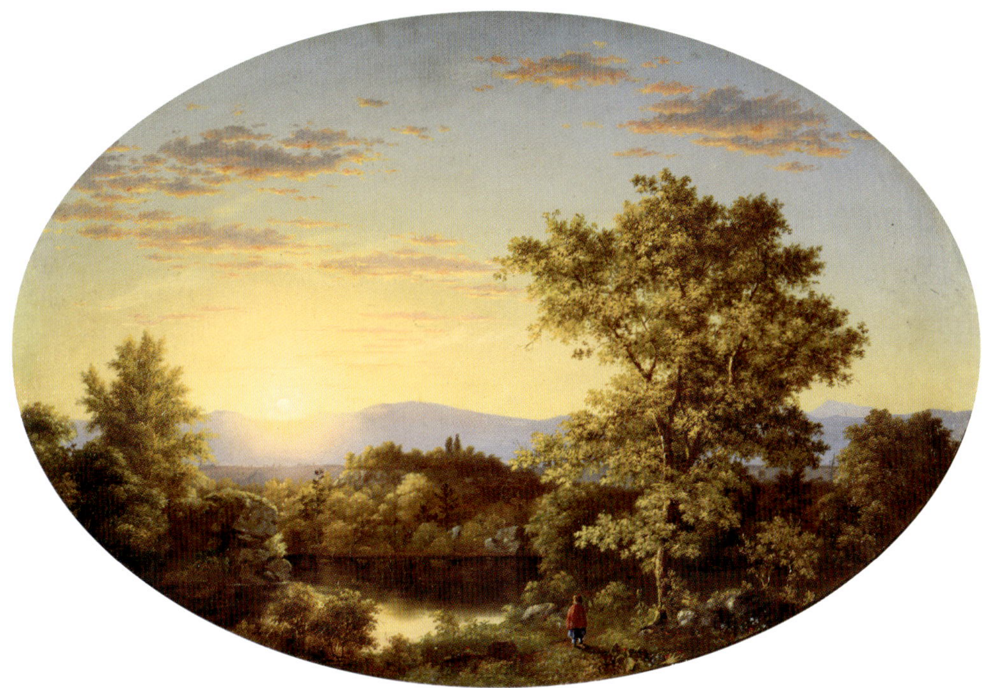

FIG. 12. FREDERIC E. CHURCH, *Twilight Among the Mountains*, 1845. Oil on canvas, 16 ¼ x 23 ½ inches. Olana State Historic Site, Hudson, New York State Office of Parks, Recreation and Historic Preservation, OL.1981.25.

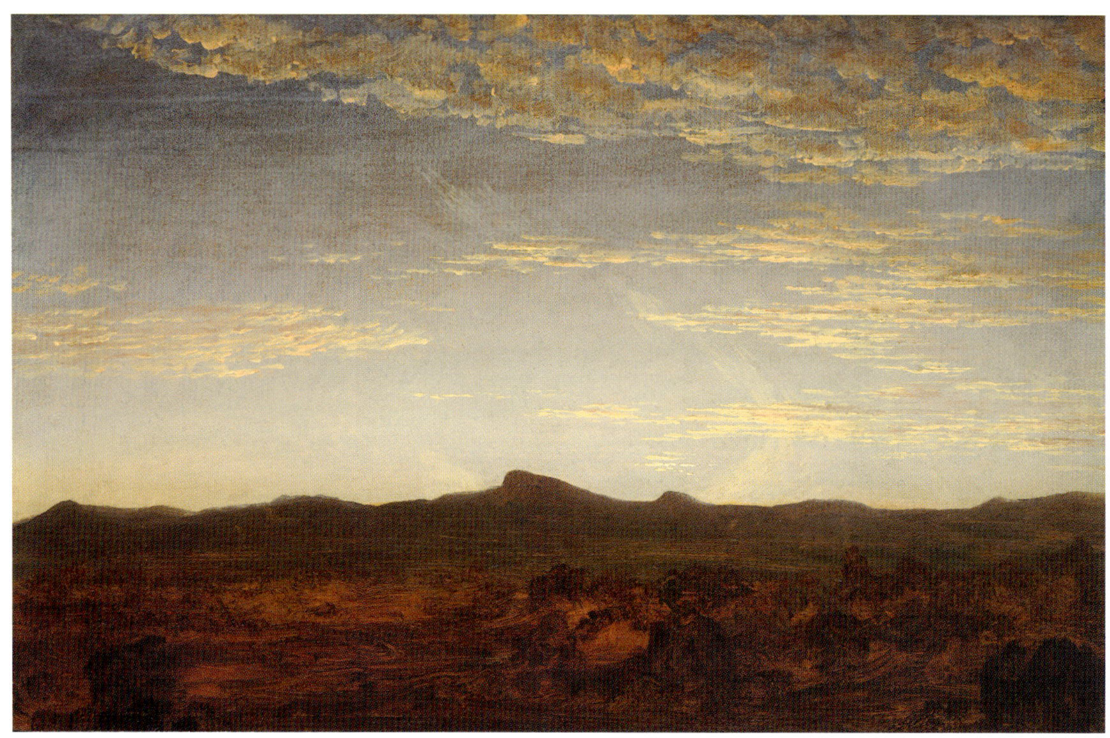

FIG. 13. THOMAS COLE, *Study for Catskill Creek*, 1844–45. Oil on wood, 12 x 18 inches. National Gallery of Art, Washington, DC.

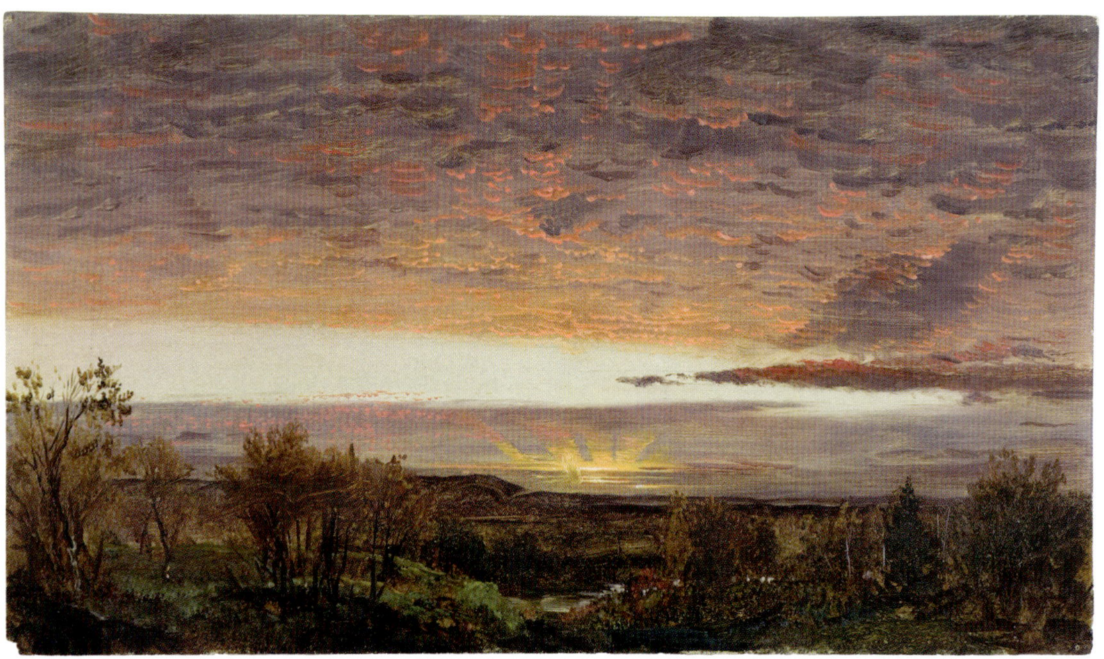

FIG. 14. FREDERIC E. CHURCH, *Sunrise*, 1847. Oil on paper, 8½ x 14⅜ inches. Olana State Historic Site, Hudson, New York State Office of Parks, Recreation and Historic Preservation, OL.1978.11.

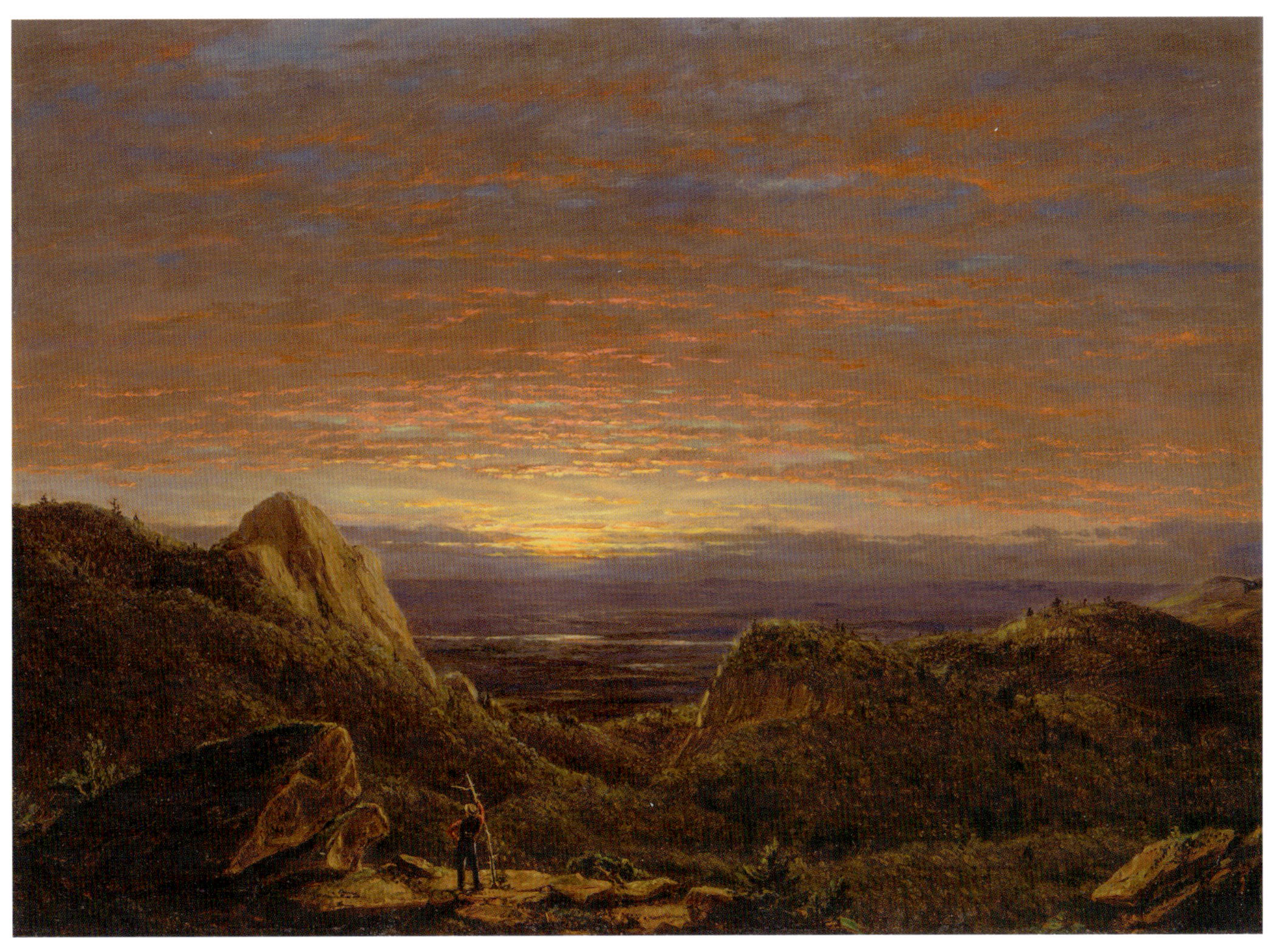

FIG. 15. FREDERIC E. CHURCH, *Morning, Looking East over the Hudson Valley from the Catskill Mountains*, 1848. Oil on canvas, 18¼ x 24 inches. Albany Institute of History and Art, NY, Gift of Catherine Gansevoort Lansing.

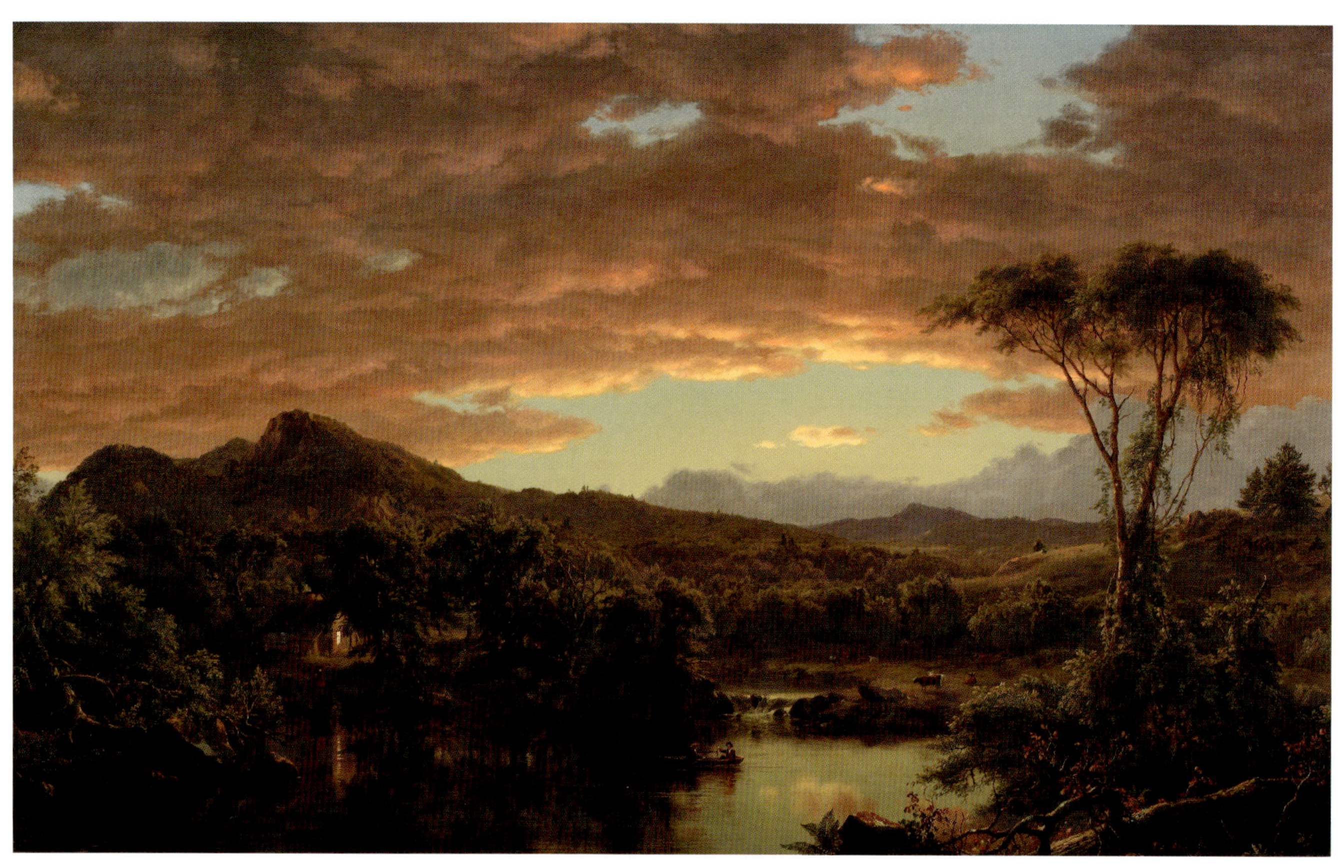

FIG. 16. FREDERIC E. CHURCH, *A Country Home*, 1854. Oil on canvas, 32 x 51 inches. Seattle Art Museum, WA, Gift of Mrs. Paul C. Carmichael.

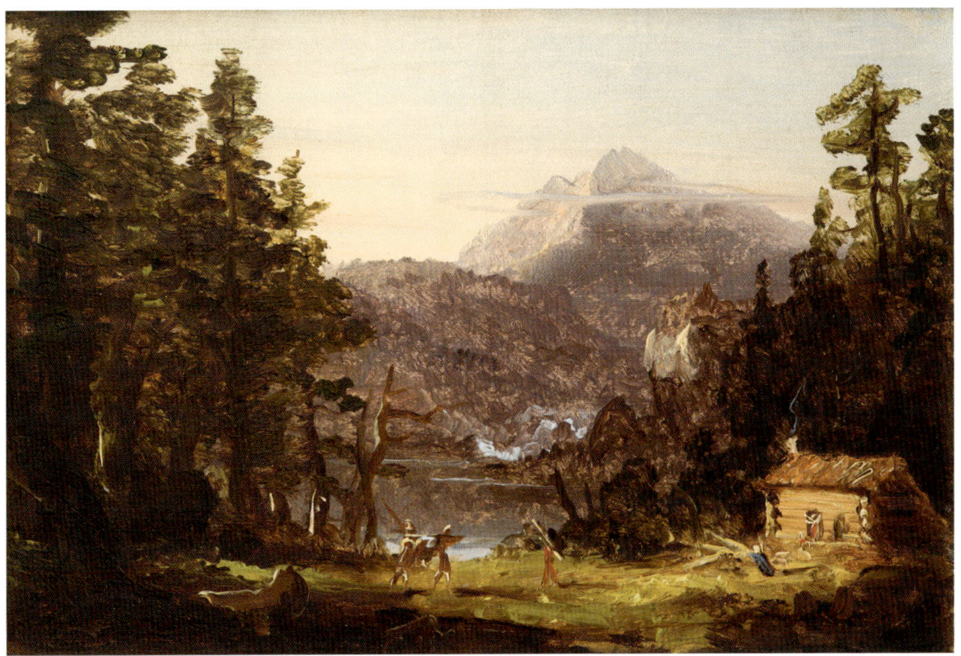

FIG. 17. THOMAS COLE, *Study for the Hunter's Return*, c. 1845. Oil on paper mounted on canvas, 7½ x 10 inches. Michael Altman Fine Art & Advisory Services, New York, NY.

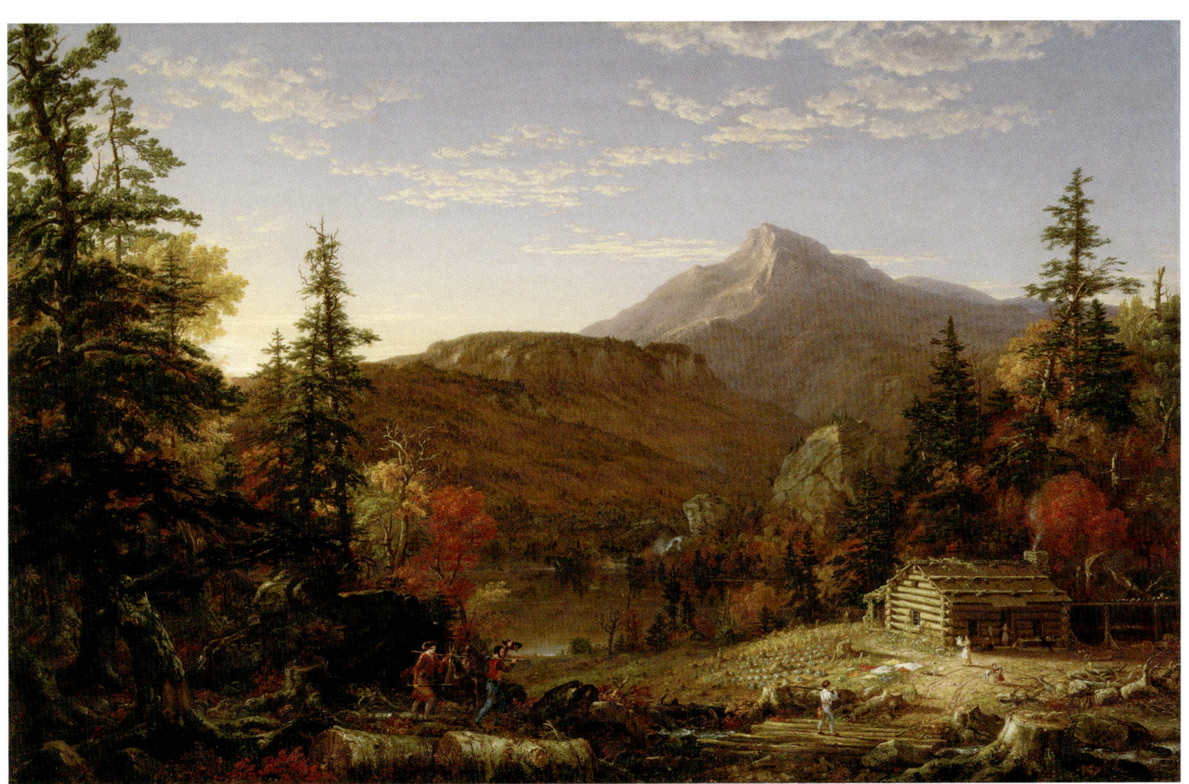

FIG. 18. THOMAS COLE, *The Hunter's Return*, 1845. Oil on canvas, 40⅛ x 60½ inches. Amon Carter Museum of American Art, Fort Worth, TX.

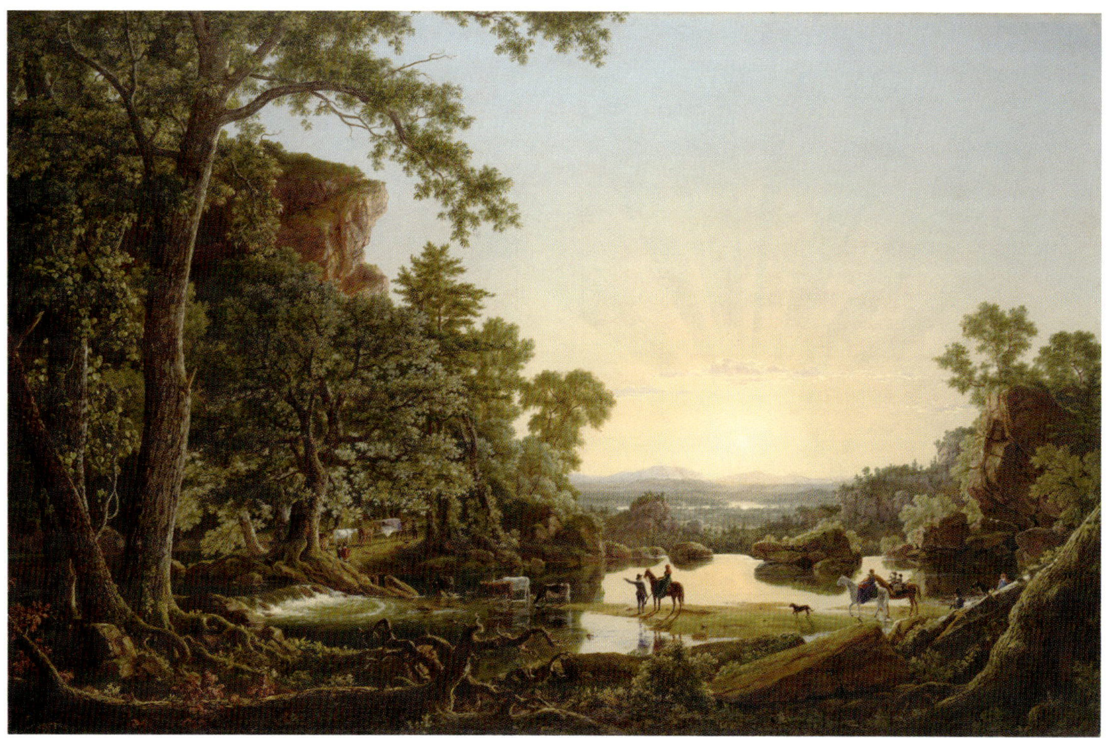

FIG. 19. FREDERIC E. CHURCH, *Reverend Thomas Hooker and Company Journeying Through the Wilderness in 1636 from Plymouth to Hartford,* 1846. Oil on canvas, 40¼ x 60³⁄₁₆ inches. Wadsworth Atheneum Museum of Art, Hartford, CT.

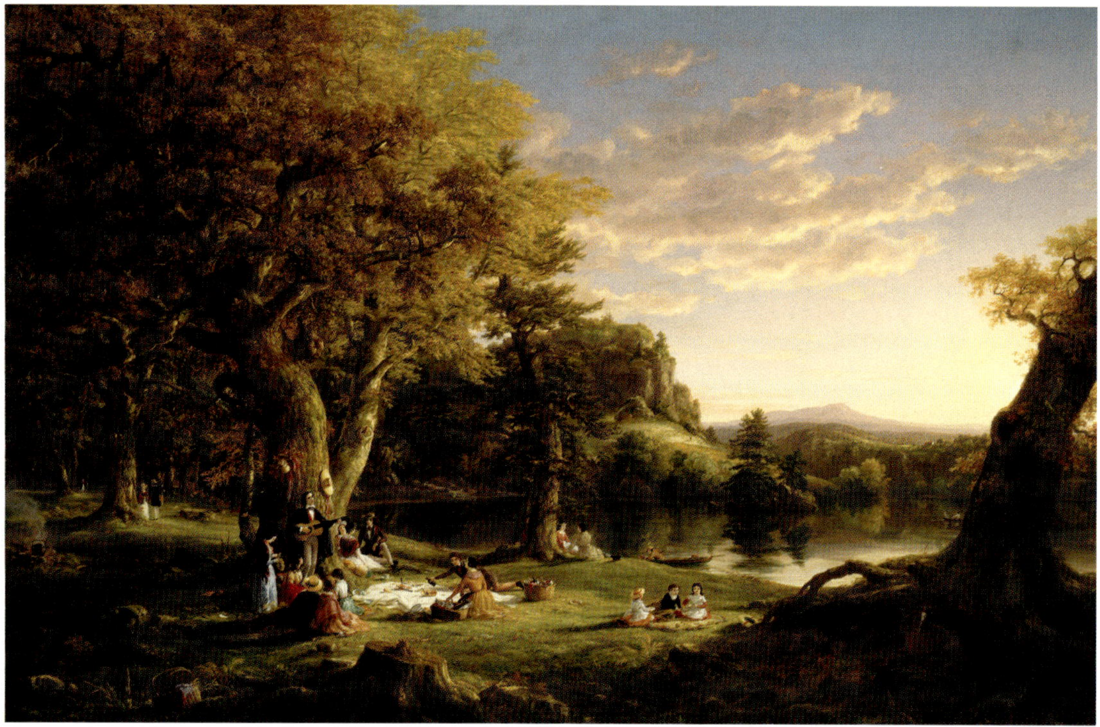

FIG. 20. THOMAS COLE, *A Pic-Nic Party,* 1846. Oil on canvas, 47⁷⁄₈ x 54 inches. Brooklyn Museum, NY.

For several years following Cole's death, from 1848 to 1854, Church picked up on his master's rendering of the simple cabin on Mount Desert in a sequence of depictions of domestic dwellings set in open nature. As Patricia Junker has demonstrated, these meditations on man and nature culminated with *A Country Home*, 1854 [FIG. 16]. Compared to Cole's works these paintings usually showed more sophisticated and comfortable farmhouses, sometimes enhanced by vivid evening skies. Church had written to his mentor on May 20, 1844, "I have frequently heard of the beautiful and romantic scenery around Catskill. . . . it would give me the greatest pleasure to accompany you in your rambles about the place observing nature in all her various appearances." [18] It is also more than coincidence that Henry David Thoreau wrote the drafts of his key work, *Walden*, during these same years. Retreating to his cabin in the woods for two years, Thoreau contemplated man's relation to nature and the various advances of industry and civilization intruding into the untouched forest.

In *Home in the Woods* and *The Hunter's Return* [FIGS. 21 AND 18] we see the pioneer's sturdy survival in the wilderness and the settlement of his family in domestic harmony with nature. On a personal level this may also be seen as a metaphor of Cole's own harmonious family life. Church picks up on this too: in 1848, the year of Cole's early death, he painted *View in Pittsford, Vermont* [FIG. 1]. Now the small dwelling in a forest clearing has evolved into a substantial country house with a two-story columned porch, extensive barn addition, and other outbuildings surrounded by a more open cultivated landscape. Early in the following decade Church continued the theme in recording farmhouses on Mount Desert, often with nearby sawmills and other evidence of productive settlement. The transformation in scenery and buildings since Cole's first example a decade earlier shows the advances in the domestication of the American landscape rapidly taking place at mid-century.

Study for a View near Stockbridge, Massachusetts [FIG. 22] and *New England Landscape* [FIG. 23] probably resulted from Church's first professional, ten-week sketching trip in the summer of 1847. Having recently completed his studies with Cole, Church visited the Lee and Stockbridge area of the Berkshires and stopped in

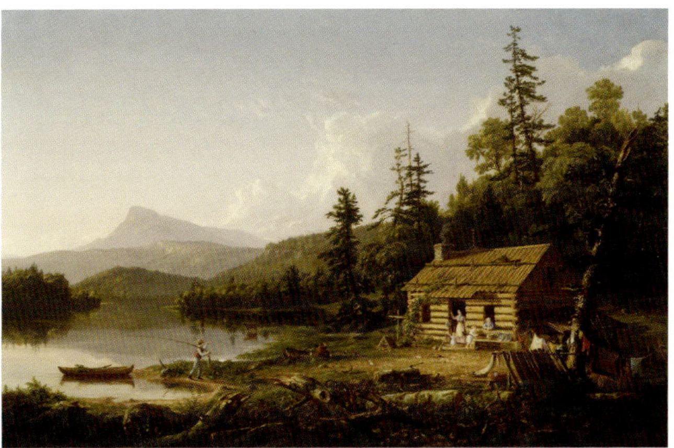

FIG. 21. THOMAS COLE, *Home in the Woods*, 1847. Oil on canvas, 44³/₈ x 66¹/₈ inches. Reynolda House Museum of American Art, Winston-Salem, NC, Gift of Barbara B. Millhouse.

Catskill that September. There are a variety of compelling observations about the works from this time. Calling upon Cole's method of composite and synthesis of landscapes, Church initially tended to combine various scenes from his travels, while on the other hand being faithful to specific details of place.[19]

Cole provided other aesthetic precedents for his pupil, some in subject matter, some in design and composition. Several historians have pointed out the older painter's use of the oval format in *The Mill, Sunset*, 1844 [FIG. 11], and its reuse by Church a year later for *Twilight Among the Mountains* [FIG. 12].[20] From his own list of possible subjects to take up Cole suggested to Church that he paint *Reverend Thomas Hooker and Company Journeying Through the Wilderness in 1636 from Plymouth to Hartford*, 1846 [FIG. 19], commemorating the early founding of Connecticut. This presented another family group, one in colonial history, but also with allusions to the biblical Holy Family's flight into Egypt. John K. Howat has further pointed out the compositional similarities between *Hooker and Company* and Cole's *A Pic-Nic Party* [FIG. 20], completed in the same year.[21] Both have towering trees rising on the left, a distant view of mountains and radiant sunlight in the right distance, and the respective families pausing or relaxing across the foreground.

At the same time Church also produced *Moses Viewing the Promised Land* [FIG. 24], a related theme owing an

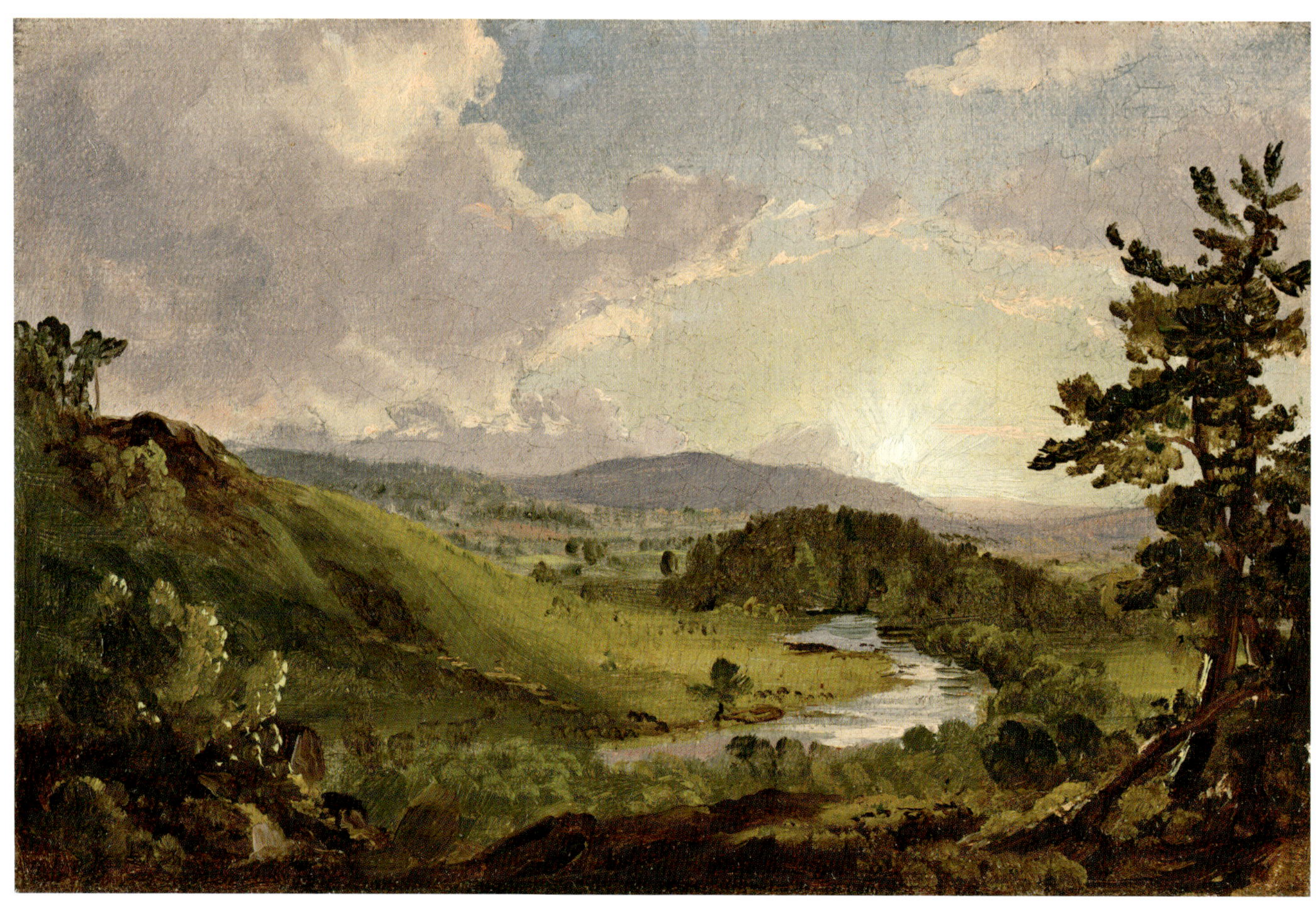

FIG. 22. FREDERIC E. CHURCH, *Study for a View near Stockbridge, Massachusetts*, 1847. Oil on board, 7½ x 11 inches. Private collection.

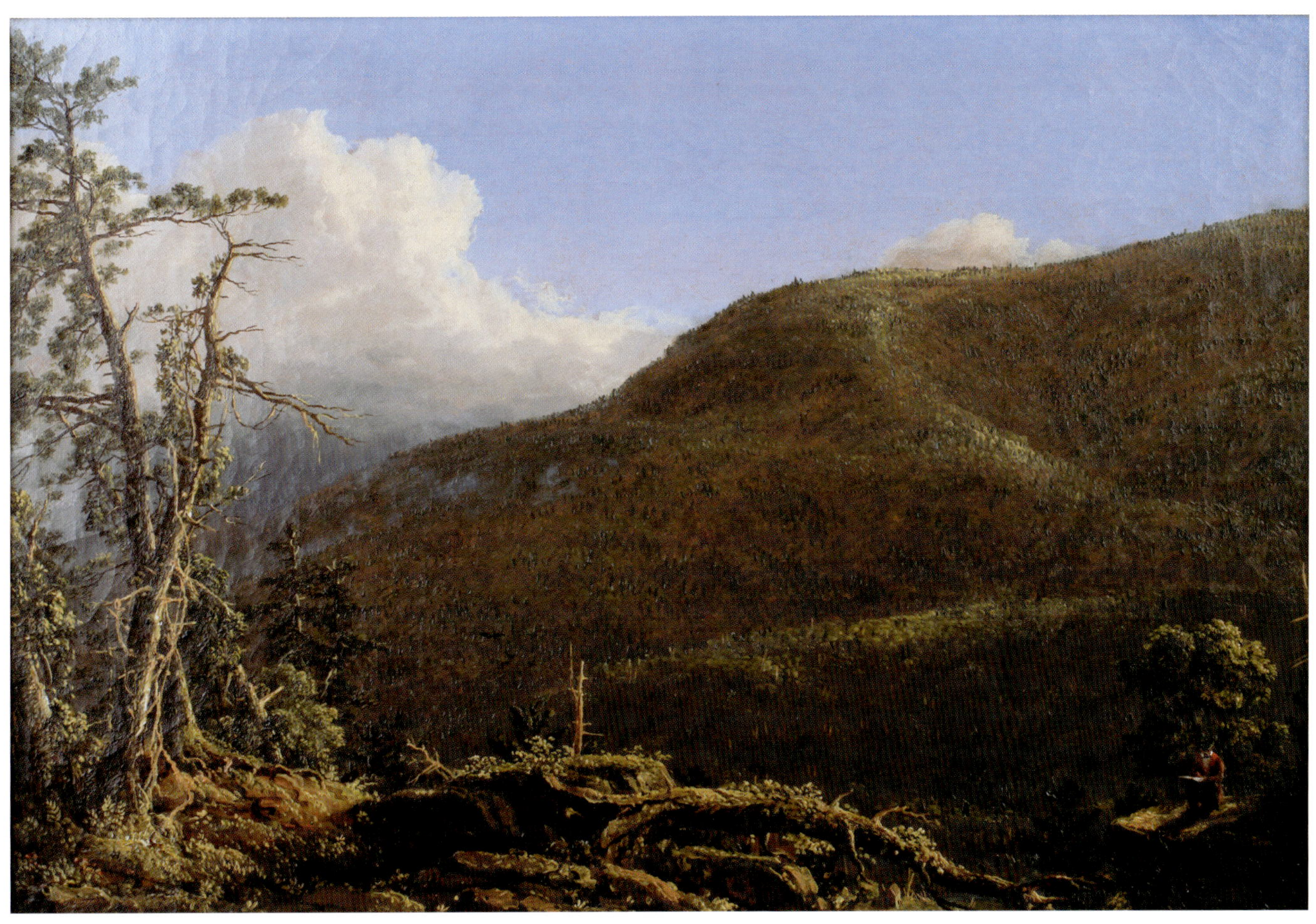

FIG. 23. FREDERIC E. CHURCH, *New England Landscape*, 1847. Oil on canvas, 14 x 20 inches. Colorado Springs Fine Art Center, CO.

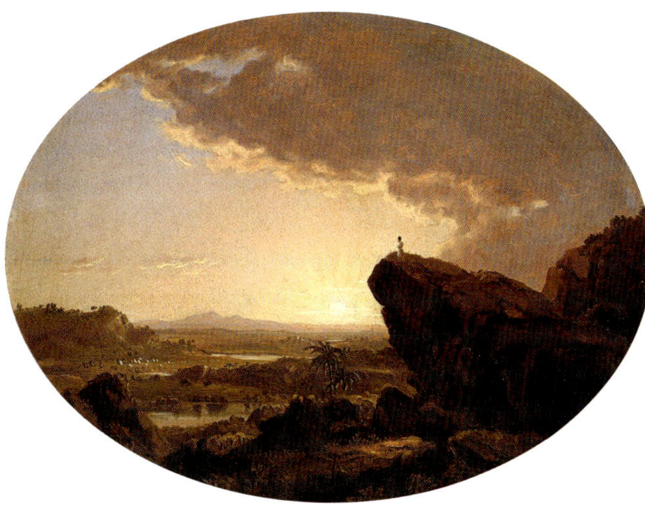

FIG. 24. FREDERIC E. CHURCH, *Moses Viewing the Promised Land*, 1846. Oil on canvas, 12½ x 10 inches. Private collection.

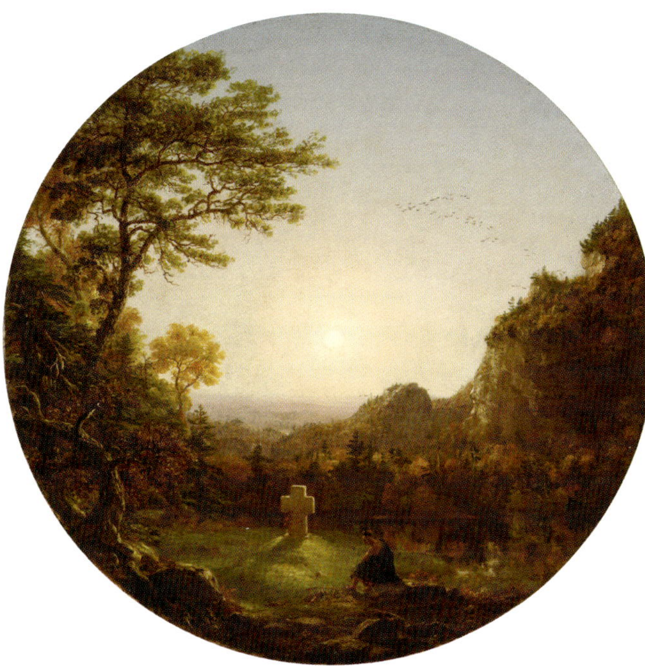

FIG. 25. THOMAS COLE, *The Cross in the Wilderness*, 1845. Oil on canvas, 24 x 24 inches. Musée du Louvre, Paris. Photo: RMN.

obvious debt to his mentor's later religious images, like *The Voyage of Life, The Cross in the Wilderness* [FIG. 25], and *The Cross and the World*. (In turn, *Hooker and Company* was to have its own reprise a few years later in George Caleb Bingham's *Emigration of Daniel Boone*, 1850, which also made respective references to the families of the artist, his historical subject, and the Bible.) Franklin Kelly additionally notes that Church's early paintings, *Christian on the Borders*, 1847 [FIG. 26], and *Plague of Darkness*, 1849, draw elements from Cole's *Expulsion from the Garden of Eden*, 1828 [FIG. 27].[22]

Some of this was the language of the sublime, which Cole knew well from his familiarity with English painting. The blasted tree trunk, for example, was in his hands evidence of God's role in nature over time. Such a tree figures prominently in *Manhood* from *The Voyage of Life* series, 1839–40 [FIG. 28]. This tree's successor dominates the foreground of Church's *Storm in the Mountains (Blasted Tree)*, 1847 [FIG. 29], though as David Huntington liked to argue, this was not a meditation on the past, but rather a recording of the present. The thunderstorm is still underway before us, and the snapped tree trunk has only freshly fallen.[23]

One important element in Cole's character during his later years, including the two spent with Church, was an abiding concern with mortality and death. In 1843 he lamented the passing of Washington Allston, a moment that "caused me to regret his loss exceedingly. He was truly a distinguished artist."[24] Allston of course had created an important body of religious history paintings, which Cole admired. But Cole repeatedly mourned the passage of time on his own birthday. On February 1, 1846, he noted, "This is my birth-day" and followed with a poem titled "The Tread of Time." Its lines included the following: "Hark. I hear the tread of time, / Marching o'er the fields sublime. / Lo! He nears us— awful Time—/ Ah, he grasps the present hour. . . . / Stop the ruffian, Time!—lay hold!—/ Is there then no power so bold?" A year later Cole again stated, "My birth-day. How they steal on!" And in 1848, as it turned out, his last, he wrote, "My birth-day. Once more the wheel of life revolved, and again advances."[25] During these years Noble claimed that Cole "prayed before he painted."

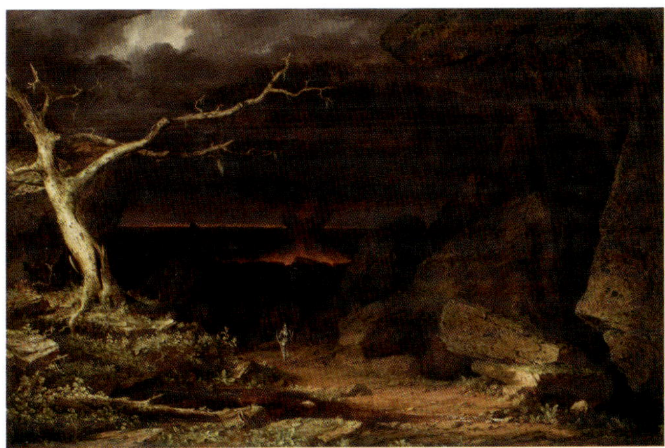

FIG. 26. FREDERIC E. CHURCH, *Christian on the Borders of "The Valley of the Shadow of Death," Pilgrim's Progress*, 1847. Oil on canvas, 40½ x 60½ inches. Olana State Historic Site, Hudson, New York State Office of Parks, Recreation and Historic Preservation, OL.1981.50.

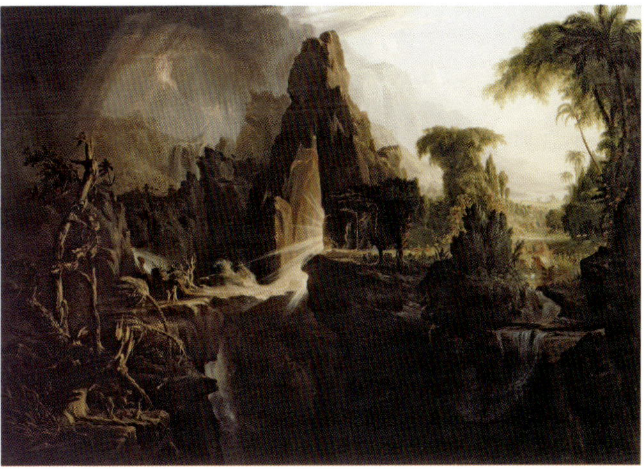

FIG. 27. THOMAS COLE, *Expulsion from the Garden of Eden*, 1828. Oil on canvas, 39¾ x 54½ inches. Museum of Fine Arts, Boston, MA, Gift of Martha C. Karolik for the M. and M. Karolik Collection of American Paintings.

Two years after Church left the Cole family, the master died. The most famous memorial painting is Asher B. Durand's *Kindred Spirits*, 1849, which depicts the painter standing on a wilderness promontory in conversation with his friend, the poet William Cullen Bryant. Church meanwhile produced *To the Memory of Cole*, 1848 [FIG. 32], with its garlanded cross in the central foreground, surrounded by a field of flowers. On one level it suggests a country tombstone; on another, the symbolic new life arising from death, a tribute to Cole's constant observation of clouds; and finally homage to one of Cole's last works, *The Cross in the Wilderness* [FIG. 25]. The crystalline draftsmanship and meteorological exactitude give the work away as explicitly by the younger artist.

Church made *View of Cedar Grove (Thomas Cole's House and Studio), Catskill, NY*, 1848 [FIG. 33], on a visit just eight months after Cole's passing. It is the most extensive and detailed view of Cedar Grove as it existed in Cole's time, and includes the main house, outhouse, and the "new studio," designed by Cole and completed December 1846 just as Church concluded his studies. Church must have deeply mourned the loss of his mentor. One can imagine the weight of responsibility that the young painter might have felt to carry on the methods and sentiments that Cole had taught him. Indeed, during the decades that follow Cole's death, Church creates a large body of work that most clearly follows his teacher's influence, and in 1860 he returns to the place where his associations first began with Cole to build his house Olana, directly across the river from Cole's Cedar Grove. Church's *Vision of the Cross, study for "Apotheosis to Thomas Cole"* and *Study for "Apotheosis to Thomas Cole"* [FIGS. 30 AND 31] present a mystery if held to the 1847 dates assigned in their accession, which clearly reference Cole's own allegorical work. Since the term "apotheosis" refers to the glorification or elevation of a figure to the level of the divine, it seems more likely these would have been painted in the years following Cole's death.[26]

If all the foregoing makes clear the pervasive impact of Cole on these formative years of Church's art, there were nonetheless emerging differences in style and execution between the two, which now require some fuller exploration. To be simplistic, trees, rocks, and clouds tended for Cole to be generalized, often carrying symbolic meaning, whereas in Church's hand they reflected greater specificity and individuality. Cole's art had been grounded in past European traditions; Church belonged to a younger generation with a rising interest in scientific observation. The former tilted toward the ideal, the latter to the real. Church saw the spiritual in nature, but was interested in recording direct human experience, not mankind in general but individuality in all species of earthly matter.

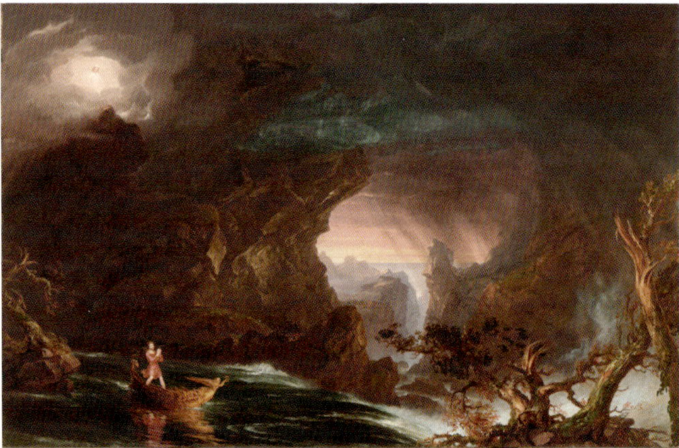

FIG. 28. THOMAS COLE, *The Voyage of Life: Manhood*, 1840. Oil on canvas, 52 x 78 inches. Munson-Williams-Proctor Arts Institute, Utica, NY. Photo: John Bigelow Taylor.

Painted in the same year as *Hooker and Company* [FIG. 19], *The Charter Oak at Hartford*, 1846 [BACK COVER], suggests the painters shared an interest in history and allegory, while also evidencing Church's unique path forward. Cole had previously sketched the historically significant tree (Detroit Institute of Art 39.307), and Church made two finished oil paintings of this tree that was rumored to be over one thousand years old. The first canvas is dated by Olana to early 1846 (Olana OL.1981.16A), while he was still a student in Catskill. The second is thought to have been made after he had returned home to Hartford. In an October 1846 letter to Cole, Church writes: "I have made a careful drawing of the 'charter oak' from a new point of view, intending to paint it on a pretty large canvas during the coming months."[27] This new vantage point, also seen in the second easel painting, still centrally features the grand tree, but the earlier view of expansive open hills and distant mountains is replaced by previously omitted signs of everyday reality—namely a long winding fence and numerous buildings that stood near it. Church had an ability to be mindful of both the symbolic and the real.

A good indication of their differences may be seen in Cole's *Mount Etna from Taormina* [FIG. 34], painted in 1843 just before his pupil's arrival, but one of the first oils the younger man would have seen in the studio. The image must have made an impression, because its composition recurs a few years later in Church's handling

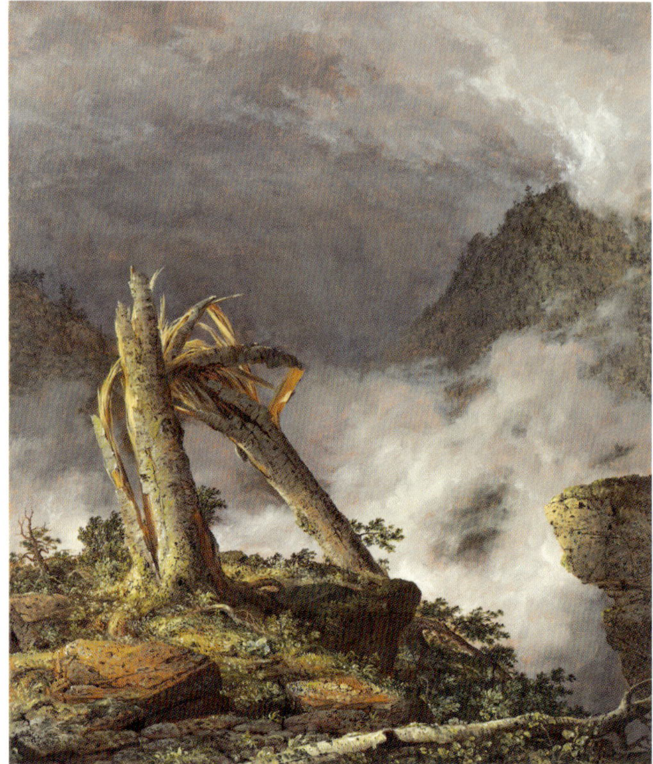

FIG. 29. FREDERIC E. CHURCH, *Storm in the Mountains (Blasted Tree)*, 1847. Oil on canvas, 75 1/2 x 62 7/8 inches. The Cleveland Museum of Art, OH.

of *Cotopaxi*, 1855 [FIG. 35]. But in place of the ancient ruins across Cole's foreground, and their reminder of past glories, the younger artist paints the New World hemisphere, where a thriving farm dwelling exists in the landscape before the volcano. In the first, the mountain represents destruction; in the latter, nature's power is evident in the wispy plume of smoke, yet tranquil within the perfect snowy cone and rendered in bright colors and cool sunlight. The earlier work displays a romantic pessimism, while the later radiates a passionate optimism. (That would change in the next decade when Church returned to the subject of Cotopaxi and showed it in lurid explosiveness during the horrific upheaval of the Civil War.)

The respective approaches of the two artists to their work are evident both in preliminary sketches and finished canvases. Carr has summarized some of their shared procedures, such as annotations accompanying drawings, white highlighting for details, occasional panoramic compositions, and of course concentration on the Catskill

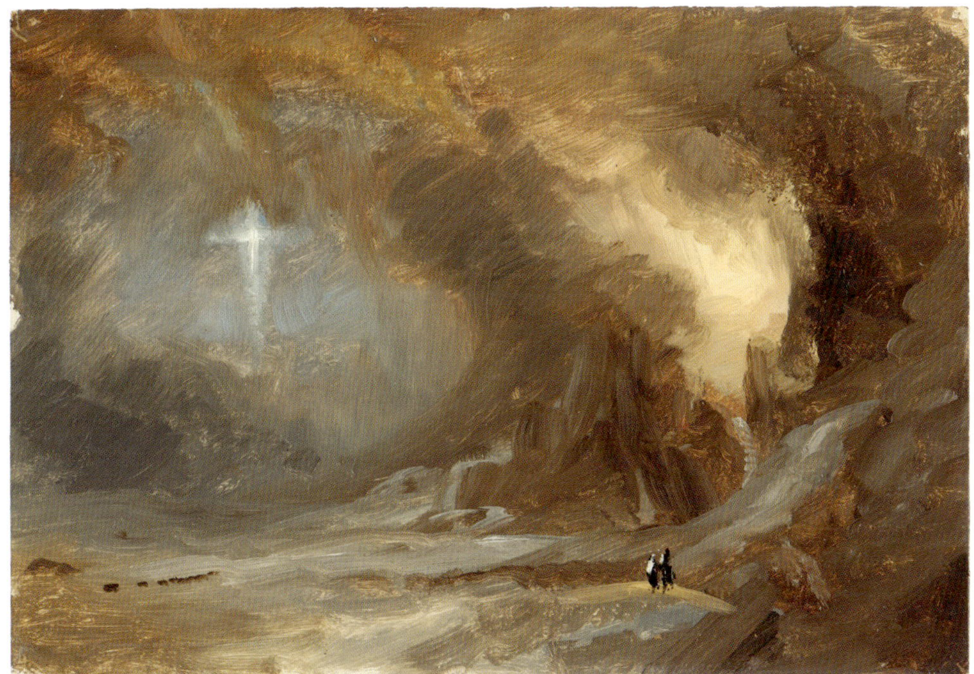

FIG. 30. FREDERIC E. CHURCH, *Vision of the Cross, study for "Apotheosis to Thomas Cole,"* c. 1847. Brush and oil paint on paper laminate, 8³⁄₈ x 12³⁄₄ inches. Cooper-Hewitt, National Design Museum, Smithsonian Institution, New York, NY, Gift of Louis P. Church, 1917-4-254-b. Photo: Matt Flynn © Smithsonian Institution.

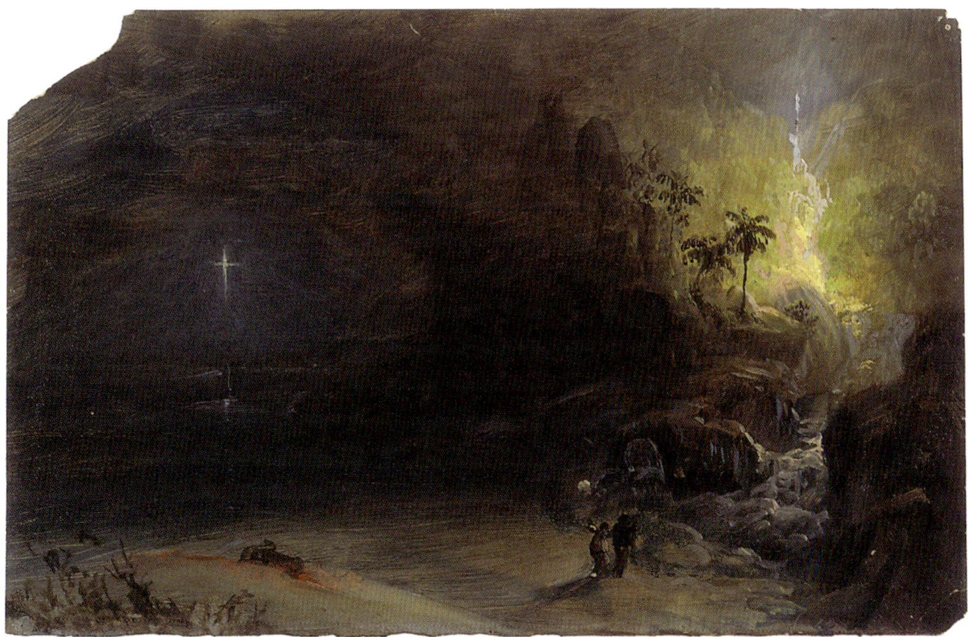

FIG. 31. FREDERIC E. CHURCH, *Study for "Apotheosis to Thomas Cole,"* c. 1847. Brush and oil paint on paper laminate, 8⁷⁄₁₆ x 12³⁄₄ inches. Cooper-Hewitt, National Design Museum, Smithsonian Institution, New York, NY, Gift of Louis P. Church, 1917-4-254-a. Photo: Matt Flynn © Smithsonian Institution.

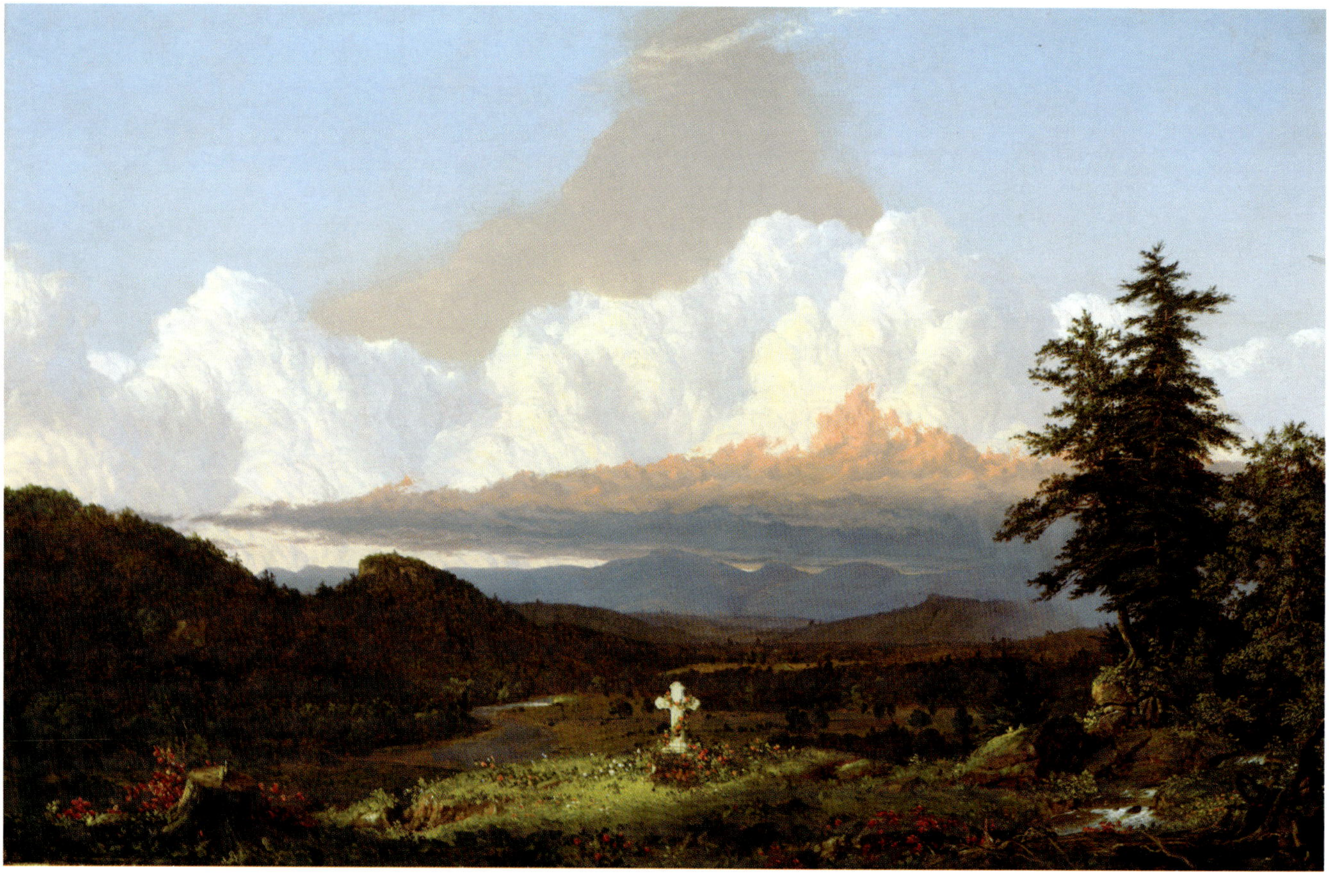

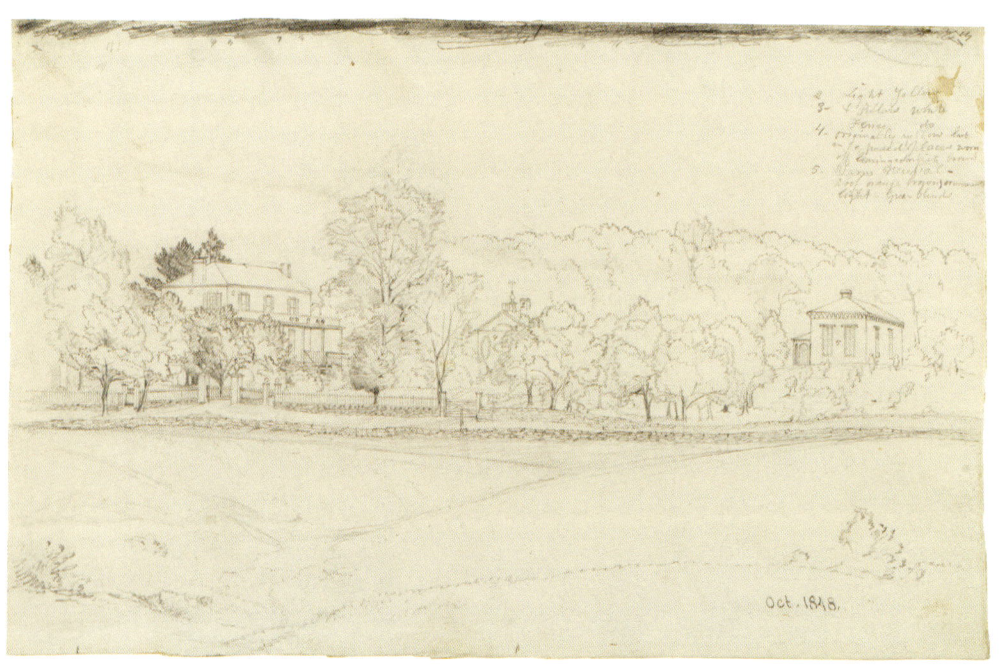

FIG. 32. FREDERIC E. CHURCH, *To the Memory of Cole*, 1848. Oil on canvas, 32 x 42 inches. Private collection.

FIG. 33. FREDERIC E. CHURCH, *View of Cedar Grove (Thomas Cole's House and Studio), Catskill, NY, 1848*, October 1848. Graphite on buff paper, 6³/₄ x 10¹/₄ inches. Olana State Historic Site, Hudson, New York Office of Parks, Recreation and Historic Preservation. OL.1980.1413.

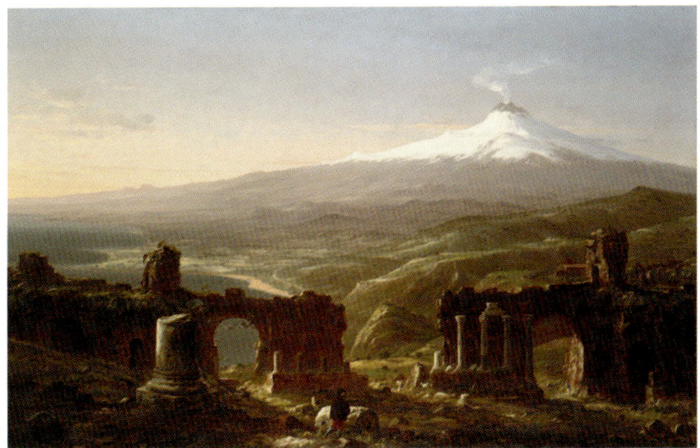

FIG. 34. THOMAS COLE, *Mount Etna from Taormina*, 1843. Oil on canvas, 78⅝ x 120 5/8 inches. Wadsworth Atheneum Museum of Art, Hartford, CT, Purchased from the artist for the museum by Daniel Wadsworth.

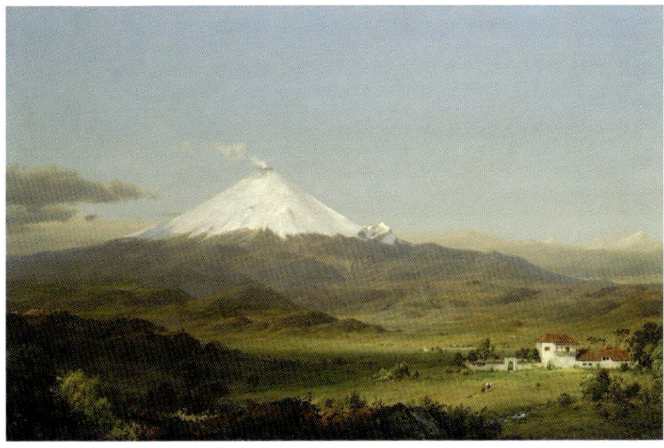

FIG. 35. FREDERIC E. CHURCH, *Cotopaxi*, 1855. Oil on canvas, 28 x 42 inches. Smithsonian American Art Museum, Washington, DC, Gift of Mrs. Frank R. McCoy.

area for subjects. For example, both visited and recorded the Catskill Mountain House on South Mountain, and we already noted several other repeated themes. But within these conventions are distinct differences. Carr describes Cole's trees as having more exaggerated, even tortured, features; they are more broadly handled and restless. In contrast, Church's are more carefully detailed, dispassionate, and sedate.[28] Although both delineated individual rocks and trees, Cole's seem more generic and expressive, Church's more specifically individualized.

The older painter often presented his trees as embodiments of larger philosophic ideas. One sheet of about 1835–40 and now in the Detroit Institute of Arts depicts a cluster of trees in the foreground seen against the Catskills profiled beyond. This he titled *Tranquility*, as if the configuration could convey a state of mind. In other instances, more contorted limbs and roots expressed a condition of emotional agitation. Both artists frequently wrote extensive notations on sketches, as well as exact times of day, effects of light, and particularities of color. However, Church's first drawings of Mount Desert in 1850 were not intended to lead to the manipulations we have seen in Cole's works, but were scrupulous statements of the actual. "One hour after sunset . . . clouds very warm, shadow of clouds, golden green reflections, rich warm yellow in fine contrast to dark bluish water." In another Church began, "Flood Tide Just Commenced,"

and added several lines of detail: "yellow and rusty light . . . very few white barnacles."[29]

Cole had articulated his own more philosophic sense of nature, and the grander role of its components beyond their mere appearance in the landscape, in the famous statement he wrote called "Essay on American Scenery." Published in 1836, it had direct parallels in the equally important essays by Emerson on "Nature" and "The American Scholar," which also appeared just at this time. Their purpose was to promote and celebrate the distinctive national and spiritual properties of the American landscape. Among Cole's early declarations was: "The wilderness is YET a fitting place to speak of God." On a different level, experiencing the landscape was a "source of delight and improvement." To these ends it was necessary for the elements of nature to be expressive to carry philosophical content, such as evidence of God's hand in the world. So for Cole to record a specific tree was too much a portrait and not sufficiently a symbol. "In the American forest we find trees in every stage of vegetable life and decay."[30] That message offered a loftier meditation on the passage of time.

Representing the approach taken by Church, and for the most part the next generation of Hudson River painters, was Asher B. Durand (1796–1886). Though a few years older than Cole, Durand outlived him by almost four decades, taking on the nominal leadership of the

New York school of artists and arriving at a much more particularized rendering of nature's face. Twenty years after Cole's essay, Durand wrote a number of letters in the art magazine *The Crayon*, in which he argued for individual distinctiveness. To his colleagues he urged, "draw with scrupulous fidelity the outline or contour of such objects as you shall select. . . . If your subject be a tree, observe particularly wherein it differs from other species."[31] To achieve fine detail Durand promoted the use of pen and pencil over looser sketches by brush in oil. Church's natural facility as a draftsman perfectly matched this attitude, and he was unusual in carrying over the precision of his drawings into oil studies executed with comparable exactitude.

We find the same parallel comparison of views in the two generations of Transcendentalists, in the writings of Emerson and Thoreau. The older figure took the more philosophical and generalized approach to nature, comparable to Cole, and saw its broader spiritual substance. "Every hour and change corresponds to and authorizes a different state of mind, from breathless noon to grimmest midnight." Also from his essay "Nature" 1836, Emerson announced, "Nature always wears the colors of the spirit. . . . Nature is the vehicle of thought." In the American landscape, "The happiest man is he who learns from nature the lesson of worship."[32] His younger friend and follower, Thoreau, in turn matches the preciseness of Durand and Church. Throughout his writings, whether in major books like *Walden*, the essays, and especially his nearly lifelong journals, there is an insistence on close observation and the habit of measurement. Notice in the following passage from an essay the differentiation of colors in trees and the particular configuration of a leaf: "Look at yonder swamp of maples mixed with pines. . . . Some maples are yet green, only yellow or crimson-tipped on the edges of their flakes, like edges of a hazel-nut bur; some are wholly brilliant scarlet, raying out regularly and finely every way, bilaterally, like the veins of a leaf."[33]

In his journal Thoreau repeatedly took note of different sunsets throughout the year, imagery that also preoccupied Church during the 1850s. As the seasons changed, the writer recorded their markers seen on his frequent woodland walks: "I noticed the button bush May 25th around an elevated pond or mudhole—its leaves just beginning to expand—this slight amount of green contrasted with its dark—craggly naked looking stem & branches." Of all the tree species, he found one to have special characteristics: "The birch is the surveyor's tree—It makes the best stakes to look through the sights of a compass. Their white bark was not made in vain."[34] But one of his most memorable studies was his survey, both literal and metaphoric, of Walden Pond: "As I was desirous to recover the long lost bottom of Walden Pond, I survey it carefully, before the ice broke up, early in '46, with compass and chain and sounding line." He discovered "the greatest depth was exactly one hundred and two feet."[35] His temperature notations were a similar form of concrete definition.

Beyond the differences in the drawings of Cole and Church, their brushwork in oil sketches and paintings also diverged with the changing tastes at mid-century. In Cole's oils his application of paint was relatively uniform across a composition, with little change in the brushwork as he moved from trees to rocks, clouds, and water. While early student works by Church share Cole's energetic paint handling and autumnal hues, such as in *Hudson River Valley Landscape with Winding Stream*, c. 1844 [FIG. 36], later in life Church meticulously learned to vary his brushstrokes for each passage, rougher for bark, nervous flicks for water surface, broader thicker swaths for boulders or ledges, and thin transparencies for the sky. His brushwork both described and almost embodied the particular elements within a painting.

Talk about a flair for paint: both artists admired the prolific career of Joseph M. W. Turner, a notable influence on numerous American painters in the middle decades of the century. Promoted widely by the critic John Ruskin, Turner's themes and effects can be found in Fitz Henry Lane, Sanford Gifford, and Thomas Moran. Cole had responded to the mythological and classical early subjects of the English landscapist, whereas Church demonstrated an awareness of the more dramatic and flamboyant aspects of later Turners. It is easy to see the legacy of Turner's numerous castle scenes in Cole's American and Italian landscapes. Also Turner's religious pictures like *The Deluge*, 1805, influenced similar Cole subjects. One finds the vast turbulence of Turner's *Snowstorm: Hannibal and His Army Crossing the Alps*, 1812, echoed in Cole's *Expulsion from the Garden of*

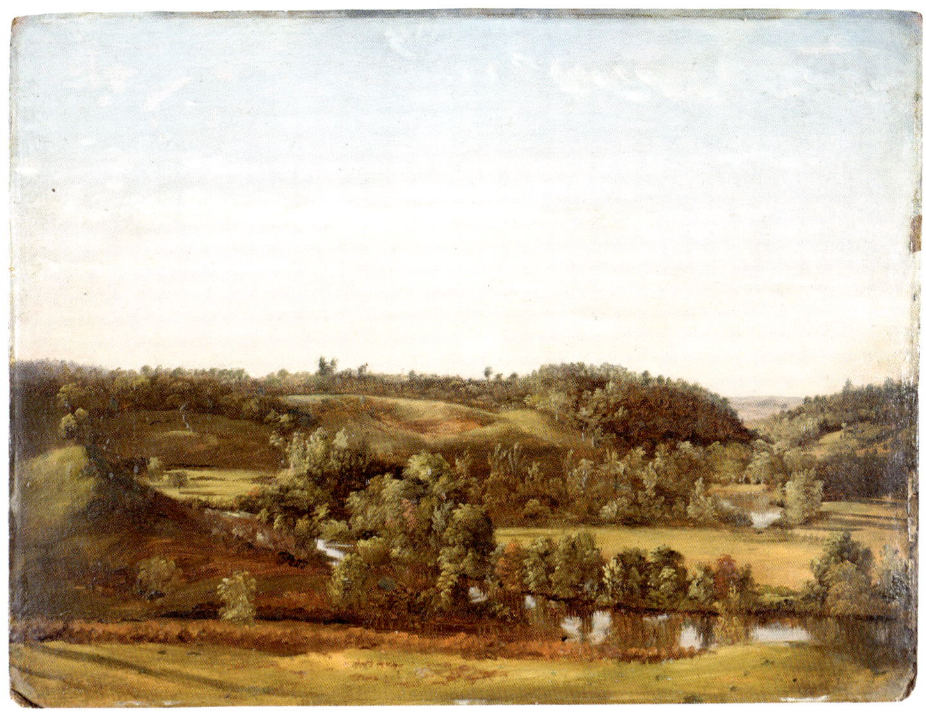

FIG. 36. FREDERIC E. CHURCH, *Hudson River Valley Landscape with Winding Stream*, c. 1844. Oil on paperboard, 12¼ x 16⅛ inches. Olana State Historic Site, Hudson, New York State Office of Parks, Recreation and Historic Preservation, OL.1981.27.

Eden, 1825, and the compositions of Turner's *Plague of Egypt* series recurring in *The Course of Empire*, 1836.

In turn, Church's many twilight scenes have a precedent in Turner's *The Lake, Petworth Sunset*, of about 1828, while the radiating fires of *The Burning of the Houses of Lords and Commons*, 1835, and *Slavers Throwing Overboard the Dead and Dying*, 1840, surely forecast the lurid explosion of Church's later *Cotopaxi*, 1863. It is fitting that twenty years after his mentor's death, Church wrote from Rome of his admiration for both Cole and Turner in poignant letters to his friend and patron William Henry Osborn: "I am more and more delighted that you have got that fine Cole—I believe him to be the best landscape painter that ever lived—If he did not have the marvellous knowledge of light and shade which distinguishes Turner's works he excelled him in color (that I will maintain before all the warmest admirers of Turner) and in profound poetic feeling he was far beyond Turner and equal to Claude and vastly superior to Claude in knowledge. Strange that the works of so great a

man should be completely overlooked. It will be my ambition hereafter to secure a fine Cole for my collection." A year later he went on, "Thomas Cole was a remarkable genius—far superior in the highest qualities to Turner—and if not quite equal to Claude in these respects—yet was so much his master in others that I feel I should prefer to own one of Cole's best landscapes—in preference to any other landscape the world can furnish."[36]

What Church had not realized was that taste in landscape painting crucially began to shift from the romantic sublime to a more down-to-earth realism in the decade following the Civil War, and would consign to the shadows not just the art of Cole but soon that of Church as well. But their time together from 1844 to 1846 was an unprecedented period of familial and artistic bonding. Moreover, Cole's influence on his apprentice continued well after Church's departure from the studio and after Cole's own death. It was an extraordinary sequence in the history of American art of an established master mentoring an emerging master.

NOTES

1. Louis Legrand Noble, *The Life and Works of Thomas Cole* (1853; ed. Elliot S. Vesell, Cambridge, MA, Belknap Press of Harvard University Press, 1964), 266–67, 270.

2. Ibid., 270.

3. Quoted in Gerald L. Carr, "Master and Pupil: Drawings by Thomas Cole and Frederic Edwin Church," *Bulletin of the Detroit Institute of Art* 66, no. 1 (1990): 48.

4. Noble, 270.

5. Ibid.

6. See John Wilmerding, "Thomas Cole in Maine," *Record of the Art Museum, Princeton University* 49, no. 1 (1990): 2–23.

7. Noble, 270.

8. Ibid.

9. Ibid., 272.

10. See Gerald L. Carr, *Frederic Edwin Church: Catalogue Raisonné of Works of Art at Olana State Historic Site,* 2 vols. (New York: Cambridge University Press, 1994), 1: 103.

11. See Franklin Kelly, *Frederic Edwin Church and the National Landscape* (Washington, DC: Smithsonian Institution Press, 1988), 36–37.

12. "The Fine Arts. Exhibition at the National Academy. Second Saloon," *Literary World,* 5 June 1847, 419.

13. Charles Dudley Warner, "Life of Church," 1899, chap. 3: 7–9 in Carr, *Catalogue Raisonné,* 1: 38.

14. Evelyn D. Trebilcock and Valerie A. Balint, *Glories of the Hudson— Frederic Edwin Church's Views from Olana* (Hudson, NY: Olana, 2009), 32–33.

15. Noble, 271.

16. Ibid.

17. Carr, *Catalogue Raisonné,* 1: 132–33.

18. Frederic Church to Thomas Cole, May 20, 1844, Cole Family Papers, Acc. # SC10635. Box 3, Folder 4. New York State Archives, Albany, NY.

19. For example, Gerald L. Carr views *New England Landscape* as scenery that mixes the Catskills with specific details from the Berkshires, whereas Kevin Avery situates this work as *Kauterskill Clove, Catskill,* the "unlocated" picture so titled at the American Art-Union in 1847. Through photographs of the site and comparison to Gifford's *View from South Mountain in the Catskills* of 1873 (St. Johnsbury Athenaeum, VT), he identifies the mountain opposite as the foot of Kaaterskill High Peak. See Carr, "Seeing the Light" in *Frederic Edwin Church—In Search of the Promised Land* (Berry-Hill Galleries, New York, 2000), 48–49, and Avery, "Gifford and the Catskills: Resort and Refuge," in *Within the Landscape: Essays on Nineteenth-Century American Art and Culture,* eds. Phillip Earenfight and Nancy Siegel (Carlisle, PA: Trout Gallery, Dickinson College, 2005), 155–57, ills.

20. Kelly, 5.

21. John K. Howat, *Frederic Church* (New Haven: Yale University Press, 2005), 15.

22. Kelly, 19.

23. David C. Huntington, *The Landscapes of Frederic Edwin Church: Vision of an American Era* (New York: Braziller, 1966).

24. Noble, 262.

25. Ibid., 274–75.

26. Carr asserts a number of reasons to date these works to 1860–61. See Carr, "Seeing the Light," 68.

27. Thomas Cole Papers, Detroit Institute of Art, in Carr, *Catalogue Raisonné,* 1: 110.

28. Carr, "Seeing the Light," 48, 50, 53.

29. Notations by Frederic E. Church on drawings (OL.1977.52 and OL.1980.1460). See Carr, *Catalogue Raisonné,* 2: Nos. 287 and 296.

30. Thomas Cole, "Essay on American Scenery," 1835, in *John W. McCoubrey: American Art 1700–1960: Sources and Documents* (Englewood Cliffs, NJ: Prentice-Hall, 1965) 100, 206.

31. Asher B. Durand, "Letters on Landscape Painting," 1855, ibid., 110.

32. Ralph Waldo Emerson, "Nature," 1836, in *The Complete Essays and Other Writings of Ralph Waldo Emerson,* ed. Brooks Atkinson (New York: Modern Library, 1940), 6, 7, 14, 34.

33. Henry David Thoreau, *The Major Essays,* ed. Jeffrey L. Duncan (New York: Dutton, 1972), 236–37.

34. Henry David Thoreau, *A Year in Thoreau's Journal: 1851* (Harmondsworth: Penguin Books, 1993), 57 (May 29, 1851), and 83 (June 22, 1851).

35. Henry David Thoreau, *Walden,* ed. J. Lyndon Shanley (Princeton, NJ: Princeton University Press, 1989), 285, 287.

36. Frederic Edwin Church to William Henry Osborn, November 9, 1868, and November 24, 1869, in the collection of Olana State Historic Site. Thanks to Valerie Balint at Olana for calling attention to these documents.

This catalogue accompanies the exhibition
*Master, Mentor, Master:
Thomas Cole & Frederic Church*
at the Thomas Cole National Historic Site
April 30–November 2, 2014

The Thomas Cole National Historic Site preserves and interprets the home and studios of Thomas Cole, the founder of the Hudson River School of painting, the nation's first art movement. Cole's profound influence on America's cultural landscape inspires us to engage broad audiences through innovative educational programs that are relevant today.

Thomas Cole National Historic Site
218 Spring Street, PO Box 426
Catskill, New York 12414
518.943.7465 | www.thomascole.org

ESSAY: John Wilmerding
DIRECTOR'S FOREWORD: Elizabeth B. Jacks
EDITOR: Kate Menconeri
COPY EDITOR: Kathleen Luhrs
DESIGN: Rita Lascaro
PRINTING: Fort Orange Press, Albany, NY

Copyright © Thomas Cole National Historic Site
ISBN: 978-0-9823444-1-5